# Consciousness and the Alien Mind

## A Spiritual Journey to Other Dimensions

## Robert Lomax

BALBOA.
PRESS
A DIVISION OF HAY HOUSE

Balboa Press books may be ordered through booksellers or by contacting:

Balboa Press
A Division of Hay House
1663 Liberty Drive
Bloomington, IN 47403
www.balboapress.co.uk
1 (877) 407-4847

Print information available on the last page.

ISBN: 978-1-9822-8095-6 (sc)
ISBN: 978-1-9822-8096-3 (e)

Balboa Press rev. date: 09/23/2019

*Dedicated to all those that have spoken with love and understanding, enabling me to peer into parts of myself and other worlds in greater clarity.*

# Acknowledgements

I would like to thank the following for their
assistance in making this book possible:

*Psychic artist* Janet Oakman
*Cover design* Chandler Book Design
*Graphic artist* Nicholas Walsh Designs
*Editor* Anne Gillion, ASG Editorial

# Contents

# Preface

## The Andromedan Perspective by Antemedi

Antemedi is an observer of humanity and, through his 'outreach role', provides unusual insights into our way of being. He outlines potential growth in mind and spirituality and gives different perspectives on our scientific understandings.

While communication already exists with several alien species, the Andromedans wish to demystify the subject. They wish to make themselves known and bring forward consciousness knowledge so that it is available to everyone.

This approach is one of many, and it has been carefully planned by one of their communication groups. The ongoing contact will continue and the level of information will increase as our society becomes more settled in its reactions and expectations.

This mental communication is open to all of us, as you will see in the following pages.

*Portrait of Antemedi as drawn by*
*psychic artist Janette Oakman*

# Introduction

We have all been told before that the mind is an incredibly powerful tool. But without knowing more of its capabilities, we are stuck in first gear altering the engine speed. Of course, it has more gears, but did you know it was capable of hyper-speed and inter-dimensional travel?

The mind is an extension of our heart and soul, not the other way round. Some people 'think' their way through life, believing feelings can be controlled by the mind. Society tends to value higher cerebral functions over the emotional. But we cannot think our way out of emotions – if we subjugate them to become an extension of the mind, we cause conflict.

Feelings and thoughts have many forms of consciousness. Feelings are not what you *think,* they are more than that.

Feelings don't just inhabit the brain, they exist in the cells of the body as well as the ethereal energies in our aura. These energetic bodies are both internal and external to the physical one. Our feelings and minds are multidimensional, and this enables them to access other dimensions and realms.

Antemedi and his colleagues will show that our thoughts and feelings can be processed differently. Because our way is natural to us, this doesn't mean it is the most beneficial way. It's difficult to think differently if our current way is entrenched, and this means we are prisoners of our own thoughts while thinking we are free. How can we begin to know or understand different thought programs if we don't understand how we presently process the things that we do?

We can only understand different ways of thinking through the ones that we have at present. And if we are shown alternative thoughts, these could be tainted and moulded to fit our existing perceptions.

Any humanoid that thinks differently to us could be misunderstood. Their looks may be a little unusual but their thoughts would certainly be alien to us. So the Andromedans and their helpers are putting great efforts into avoiding that.

You may be surprised to learn that there is much ongoing contact with many of us. Because this takes place upon our multidimensional soul levels, we are not fully aware of it.

To assume there is no contact with other alien cultures could not be further from the truth.

**Robert Lomax**

# ONE

Antemedi gives some background to his understandings. He explains that knowing the way we think enables him to know much about us. He provides a brief insight into our development and evolution, which currently excludes consciousness and inter-dimensional involvement. This leads into our soul connections with other entities.

## Antemedi and you

"Hello, I would like to get to know you," or as we Andromedans say, "Conapaney."

That may sound odd when you were probably thinking you would like to get to know me, particularly as I am the one reaching out to you. In any event, there are so many of you, how could I possibly know you as a separate individual?

That depends upon the definition of *'you'*. Most of you know and accept that you plug into your earthbound collective consciousness. It is a consciousness that reflects and adapts to your thoughts and feelings. As an extension of *you*, it includes each and every one of *you* that contribute to it. It is you; it is your neighbour and the whole world. It is singular and plural at the same time. It is one or the other depending on how you look at it. If I am connecting to it – it is me as well as *you* the many. Thus I am aware of the many, the totality or the few if I wish. I know *you* well, but there is always more to know.

I am part of a group that has specifically studied other cultures. We have our own school of learnings. I do not use

1

the word 'teachings' because we learn or become aware in different ways to you [1](see References for link to *Students of Life* article). You might like to think of us as an 'evolving university group'. We research and provide guidance for contact with other races. This does not impinge upon the free will of anyone to interact with you in the way they wish. The guidance is given in love and is accepted as information that can be used. Our prime objective is to understand humanoids to the best of our ability before encountering them. Though that's not always the case.

So, we can know *you* by knowing how you think and what makes you think the way that you do. There are certain elements that are common to the way you process things. You choose from a range of possibilities and formulate your own program, which gives you your modus operandi, personality and individuality. You may not fully appreciate how we can claim to know you so well – in some cases, know you better than you do – the *you* as the plural, which still contains the singular being you the reader.

In addition, we are also connected to many of you at higher soul levels. We have a union and communication there. At those levels, we are some of you and some of you are us. But who is who and what does this mean for you in your plural or singular? I have a perspective on this and I am happy to share it with you.

Robert says existing contact between humans and aliens already exists. much of which is at soul and mental levels. However, your governments have secret space programmes and have direct communication with different species. The amount of contact is hidden from the populous. You have plenty of researchers and experiencers on earth who are well versed in a wide variety of alien facts. I will not add to those

2

for it would distract me from my purpose.

Part of my outreach is to show each of you what communication you are capable of as individuals and how you may interact with us. Some of those ways I will mention in due course. Before undertaking them, reading to the end of the book will be useful.

If you accept you are a full part of the wider 'us universe', this will allow you to feel you are a member of a much bigger family. This may help when we talk about co-created relationships and a brief synopsis of your unknown history.

I believe the level of these explanations has been set so that no one is excluded from understanding them. Every person who reads this material will have different capabilities, and I am conscious not to lose anyone while explaining my perspectives. At the same time, I hope it will be stimulating for those who are more familiar with other alien disclosures. I can, however, promise some new insights for them. The aim is: *to advance communication and benevolent interaction with other cultures.* We can do this with you because we have connected mutual pasts and futures.

So, introductions and aims completed; perhaps we should look at your initial thoughts. After all, I did claim to know your ways for many reasons!

The subject of contact with aliens comes loaded with many preconceived ideas. Your first thoughts are likely to be where is the proof that I actually exist, and is it really me talking to you? It is a very valid question that should rightly be asked.

Proof may seem to be a simple yes or no. You see it or don't see it, experience it or don't experience it. Consensus beliefs are not proof for or against alien existence. While there are a few physical contacts, the majority of experiences are mental and emotional. How many individual accounts will there need to be to make facts tangible? Perhaps no figure will suffice because it is still not your proof – not your individual experience. If you put aside your personal need for proof, can other people be believed?

The problem with that is it takes us back to 'believing' as a method of proof again. The current consensus is not helpful, either – it both accepts and disregards those that have alien experiences. Ultimately, it is your personal choice to accept or reject other people's experiences.

None of what I have said is proof – what can be measured and against what? Should proof be 'apparent truth', which your media informs you according to their agenda? Perhaps mass sightings – but you have already had these. Why should so many people lie about personal experiences? Is it a phenomenon in the collective consciousness, a deeply held desire for more, or is it a glitch in your program?

Perceptions and interpretations are involved when you look for truth. If I am sad, could I prove that to you? You will perceive me by using as many of your information receptors as possible. You would look at my demeanour, my face and perhaps the way I hold myself. An understanding of my circumstances and the reasons why feel this way would help. I say I am sad, and the supporting information appears to support this. Because you compare it to your own experiences of sadness, you accept that I am sad. You have used your comparable feelings and knowledge on the inside of you, but it is not proof that someone else is sad. You superimpose your personal judgements and, on balance, accept it as proof.

You may empathise and your 'heart will go out to me'; this will create a deeper emotional experience for you but the emotional intensity can cause a blindness. It's happening to you and it's your reaction to me, but it is not actual proof of my feelings. It's compelling enough and it might be a truth. What I am saying is, I cannot prove to you what I am thinking or feeling.

You can interpret and make your own conclusions based upon the general context. But even that is incumbent upon what you think as a weighted balance. The feeling of truth is something that can be trusted but only you can gauge that. So I hope you will begin to feel that through the experience of encountering me and the others who will participate in this communication. As I speak 'in Robert' – he is typing my words to you – the words that flow are mine as if they are his. I share my sight and my experiences with him as if we are the same *you* as each other.

The credibility to trust what you feel as an 'inner knowing' depends on your experience and use of that as a sensor. This inner knowing is an attachment to the soul and the *Isness of all*. That which is untrue shows itself against the light. It cannot cloak itself in that which it is not. When you exclude beliefs, answers seem to be as much about perceptions and receptors as anything else. In your search for truth and credibility, you might like to consider the following:

- *The totality or amount of information I am making available.*
- *The gravity and unusual detail of what is provided.*
- *The cohesive way of looking at the universe, science, mind and soul.*
- *The clear distinctions between the thinking of humans and other benevolent aliens.*

## Who are 'you'?

History can give a background to alien-human connections. It can be used as a backdrop or curtain upon which to view some of my perspectives. Your history is, however, very different from what you have been told.

Earth has been colonised by humanoids for longer than you think. Your human DNA is made up of contributions from 23 different alien species. You are looked upon by many other races as having a grand heritage and huge potential in all areas of life.

There are jumps in evolution that cannot be explained by Darwinism alone. That is a theory based upon the relationship of certain pieces of information. Echoing my previous words, Darwinism it isn't proof of who you are and how you got here. It is a theory that disregards mind, consciousness programs and other universal energies [2](see References for the link to *Plausibility* article).

Smatterings of your history remain like shadows in different cultures: cataclysmic events; the end of the Golden Age; fallen angels (large humanoids); bird people; hieroglyphs and carvings of strange objects; handed-down stories of the gods in the skies carried by chariots (the spacemen in their ships). The amount of information is overwhelming and it is a well-documented subject.

It is covered by many authors, some of whom have direct alien contact. Part of this history covers the descent of man and the reduction in the number of DNA strands to two. Not only does DNA provide information to form the body but it also exists, simultaneously, as an energetic receiver and transmitter.

Wisdom, understanding and inter-dimensional faculties were lost. There was manipulation of man's psyche by 'regressive entities'. The earth became toxic with negative energies of fear, hatred and power. So, it was quarantined in an energetic shell to protect other parts of the Milky Way. Humanity reinforced its negative energy through its deeds, which darkened the collective consciousness. Humanity was culpable in creating negative energy, so it had the responsibility to face the residues and work through them generation by generation. Unfortunately, some still continue to create negative energy. Many of you call this earth 'karma' – though that is a very simple understanding because negative possibilities do not need to be energised when you see them for what they really are.

This is a very brief historical backdrop. I have only provided it to give a flavour of the fact you are not who you believe you are. However, your world is evolving and changing energetically and physically. There are challenges and birthing pains ahead as some of these old ways are thrown off. The containment fields are reduced and the part of the galaxy you now travel through provides enriching energy waves.

These energy waves are vibrational but not as you may imagine them. They are information and mental programs that affect everyone – the collective consciousness, plants, animals and earth.

A tipping point will be reached, producing a major upgrade in consciousness and physicality. At the moment, mental energetic vibrations are becoming less dense so more people are awakening.

As they wake up, their psychic abilities increase. This will help more minds and hearts reach into other realities telepathically. These are some of the reasons why so many races are taking an interest in your evolution at this time.

This is only a linear history and a physical description of what is, in reality, your mentally created holographic world. To the linear description, you will need to add reincarnation and the multidimensional nature of soul.

You have much wider connections with the universe and to

other beings than you realise. Many of these beings have unifications at deep soul levels with you.

## Soul connections

Have you ever wondered about the nature of soul – the nature of you? You may have a concept in your mind but it will be a variation of ideas postulated over a long period of time. Some ideas are distorted by ideology and religions. Entrenched views exist, and there is wacky as well as enlightened spirituality.

Proof of soul can be illusive at lower levels, so the exploration of it is only as definitive as you decide it is. You interpret my perspective in your own way because you see it through the autonomy of the individual. You believe you are 'fully individual', but that is a feeling, existing in isolation from the completeness of soul. The over-arching or wider soul is so diverse that it encompasses all.

When viewed from separation, the greater unification of soul can feel like a loss of self – the consumption of individuality and the existence of you. Coping with the 'I am you and you are me' in its fullness is a strange concept. It is an outside perspective of the inside while you experience isolation from it. The veil of forgetfulness and the constraints of linear time also hinder your 'full knowing' of soul.

My perspective is based on personal experiences. I interact with inter-dimensional aspects of myself and I talk and commune with highly evolved entities. These are not beliefs that exist within my culture but understandings, as we live and experience them in that way. Knowing the origin of the information is useful because it can show a bias or purpose. Everyone's standpoint has a bias.

What you think about depends upon your sponsoring

thoughts some of which you do not see. Like proof, truth and unbiased perspective can be illusive. It would be good if you could say that you trust yourself, but can you do so implicitly or are you filled with conflicting doubts?

For me, trust in myself and the soul is not an issue. I know myself in greater fullness and I do not need to use doubt in the same way that you do. I live in a community where I have no need to distrust. We have a way of knowing when truth does not exist. We have no need to hide or take advantage of someone else. Trust is a knowing within the heart that leads us on.

You may believe there are degrees of trust or love, but that is measurement or comparison. True love is beyond measure. Your heart at the depth of soul knows all and it can be trusted beyond the need to believe. At those levels of soul it exceeds trust – it 'just is'. We use the word 'Isness' as the totality or composite of the connected 'just is'.

The autonomy of self is a matter of perspective. Your understanding of autonomy is limited to what you are able to conceive and accept. We do not have fixed viewpoints and we are more fluid, which allows us greater closeness to the Isness. I will explain this in greater detail when I talk about our minds.

Many of you will be familiar with the words *higher self* and *over-soul* perhaps as some form of personal god-self or the seat of your soul. Your soul, however, is not the single individual that you think it is. You are one part of a twin flame – there is another part of you in the opposite sex having an experience separate to yours. Hermaphrodite union has split in order to have individuation experiences as male and female. Take a moment to imagine what it might feel like to be a unified male and female – two energies as one. Is it absorption of more to

9

you or is it the loss of you into another? Where is your autonomy, identity and individuality? In reality, it is all those things and none of them. It is all a matter of which perspective you look from. At the moment, you are looking from the individuated you.

We can go a little further down the rabbit hole. Higher self or over-soul projects itself as six hermaphrodites (twelve individuations male and female) to its make-up. There are twelve higher selves in a Monad and 144,000 Monads in a soul group. That figure some of you have heard before in religious teachings. There are, of course, many soul groups, and there are no limitations in reaching higher dimensions. Communication exists between all the aspects of soul. Which part you feel you are is a matter of singular or higher multiple focus. I do not have a singular fixed perspective so you might think my fluidity allows me to live with the loss of identity. It's not a loss, it's more a way of accepting my multidimensional nature and perspectives. I am still me but my definition of me is different. The definition of you we touched on earlier needs fluidity added to it. When you connect to these other aspects and higher levels, you will be able to share wisdom. At the moment, it may be difficult to feel the fuller self that you are. It may be more comfortable for you to see 'other aspects' of your soul as 'someone else'.

Higher vibrating soul self can be sensed or seen as 'light bodies'. This is the light of soul on ever-increasing levels of love, wisdom and potential. You are a soul and you are multidimensional. That's not easy to conceptualise until you become co-conscious of the greater fullness. Past lives and reincarnation are somewhat easier to accept because they are part of a linear progression, something you are familiar with. The past doesn't compromise the current idea of individual self but as soon as you add 'future self' to the mix, that can be unsettling. Who is who, what definition are you and when? Yes, when? Because a 'future you' can talk to a 'past you' and change the energy of that timeline. These fluid relationships you have with your soul are unknown to you.

To grasp this more easily, we will need to explore the energetic and holographic nature of soul and universe. Before we do so, you are probably beginning to join the dots together and see that Robert and I share experiences. We are parts of the same soul and we share energies. He has had experiences of other worlds in other humanoid forms including Andromedan, some which I have shown him.

Our soul (he, I and the composite) chose to help itself by undertaking a retrograde experience on earth. But, like many others, it became karmically attached to the earth, needing to reincarnate several times to expunge and clear the negative energy it created. The soul can have as many experiences as it wishes, including what you might consider to be negative ones. On earth, this is compounded by the veil of forgetfulness and the collective consciousness, so it's very easy to slip into repeating the same old patterns. Because of these difficulties and your detachment, spirit guides provide mental and emotional guidance to help you navigate the earth plane. Some people can sense or hear them while to others are they are unperceivable and become viewed as no more than their own thoughts. They are usually thought to be discarnate and between lives, which is a comforting way to think of them.

I followed this format with Robert until he was able to accept me not only as alien but also as part of our soul expression. The words he types now are mine, and he is able to accept that I am him without causing any problems. He is not subservient to me nor am I to him.

That said in my role of this particular life relationship, I have greater awareness, wisdom and foresight. I can say such things without boasting – that's just how they are. He does seek advice sometimes and I have to be careful what I say to maintain sufficient degrees of free will. We can have quite lively discussions where he will argue against my viewpoints. His questions can, at times, dictate the direction we move in and slow up the delivery of my insight. Yet he loves and trusts me beyond doubt so when I say, "It's time to listen; don't question," he does. In this way, he receives a different answer to a question he hadn't thought of. This means I can also reveal parts of his psyche, which contain the sponsoring thoughts.

His frustrations can spill over at times, yet my demeanour is unaffected. I have never yet lost an argument nor have I won one. There is no winning or losing, only variations in perspective from different vantage points. It is the different perspectives that I am revealing. I do not stumble I am more connected to the 'Isness' than he, and I have easier access to different levels of higher collective consciousness. I am instantly available to him because my consciousness works on several levels at once. I can say all these things because it is just how things are. Just is!

If you had a sudden energetic opening and saw alternative realities, it would take a while to become accustomed to it. If an alien being said that it was you, that might appear as a form of psychosis to other people.

So, there are several steps of self-reconditioning needed before for these multidimensional perspectives could sit comfortably with you. Only when you leave present understandings on the doorstep can you consciously walk over a threshold into different vibrational realities.

You are likely to have many questions. Why is this alien

information coming out now? What does this mean for your individuality and autonomy? If you are to be more, what is the totality of you? Where have you been before and what have you experienced?

Thoughts expand exponentially and the mind can trip from one mental possibility to another. This would be searching to find meaning and substance. It is a desire to collate or match what I have said against your existing understanding and database. But they cannot be answered in the present way you resolve problems because there is no match to your current data.

Comparisons and measurement will be ineffective. You will need to exceed measurement and see soul essence and its part in the multidimensional universes.

## Nature of reality and its relationship to soul

All the subjects I and other presenters talk about are intrinsically interconnected. I cannot separate sentience from science or soul from mental and emotional vibrations. Everything is linked with consciousness programs, which work upon different vibrational levels. You might compare the word 'program' to your use of computer technology, however, you will need to include consciousness and entity. Different programs run different aspects of your life including your body function. Consciousness programs underpin creation and matter in the different densities and dimensions of the universe.

I am not giving a technical description for your concept of God the creator. You could use it that way if you wish. That would be to superimpose your words and understandings over mine. We look at things differently to your god concept, as you will come to see. There are many types of programs and some of them you would be quite surprised to learn about. For example, our technologies and engineering have a level of conscious awareness.

Our crafts do not use electrical circuits in the same way that yours do. They have a consciousness that we interact with and, in this way, the craft becomes an extension of our thoughts and of ourselves. Many of you associate sentience as individuals having soul, mind and consciousness. That needs to be revised to include things like your planet earth because, while it is a program, it is also conscious and it is sentient. Like you and me, it is also multidimensional –vibrating at different rates in different dimensions.

Sentience means something different to Andromedans, so making comparisons from your existing database will slant the information.

We can also say you are an extension of the earth's consciousness and it is an extension of yours. To be sentient with soul requires both separation and union. Higher realms would show your reality as being 'the appearance of separation' played out upon different levels of consciousness.

Humans' group and collective consciousness is not the only one on your planet. Animal consciousness, herd instinct, insect hive levels of consciousness are but a few. Bird flight patterns, homing instincts and even the growth of plants and flowers are part of a system of consciousness. At times, the words consciousness and programs seem interchangeable, though there is a tendency to associate consciousness with sentience. So, there are many different levels and types of programs. They can also allow quick changes or longer adaptations. Programs exist everywhere, from the smallest of particles to the very universe itself – from free-flowing thoughts to complex beings. We will show you other diverse programs as we move forward. Now, however, I would like to show you the basic building blocks of dimensions and matter and their part in programs.

**Information fields:** This is a term we use instead of *program*. Program and information are not the same things. Information fields also create a good metaphor in your mind's eye. They give not only a grasp of the beautifully complex *'potential'* laid out before you but the description gives a feeling that is tangible. The information can be dormant or active. There is potential for everything, but only that which suits the information of the program is used, otherwise matter would be unstable.

**Pulse energy:** This is the underlying energy; once created, it became self-sustaining. We will talk about 'initial origin energy' later. Pulse energy is a high-intensity fluctuation. It goes from off to on and off and on again, repeatedly. The energy is here and not here – created and not created. It may take a while to get your head around this. It is not easy to conceive that we all live in worlds that are 'here and not here at the same time'. Your experience tells you that your world is solid when it is actually fluid and in constant flux. The fluctuations are so fast that they are unseen without the use of advanced technology. Because we vibrate faster, we can also use our minds to look into solid objects and see them at their energetic levels. Solid is energy and what you see is 'the way you see'; it is how you are used to seeing it in your reality.

**Harmonies:** As the pulse energy fills or ignites the information fields, energetic harmonies occur – resonances if you like. This you know from singing with someone else; when you hit the same pitch, your vibrations will match. The sum of your vibration modulates, increasing the intensity. This example, however, is only supplied to give you a feeling of what is happening. I do not wish to compare modulating or sine wave energies (oscilloscope: up-and-down waves) with pulse 'on-off' energies. These harmonies interact with other harmonies that have been created in the same space. So, we have the collision or the formation in the same space of several harmonies. A while back, we showed Robert bubbles of harmonies, which he painted in order to show these points of intensity.

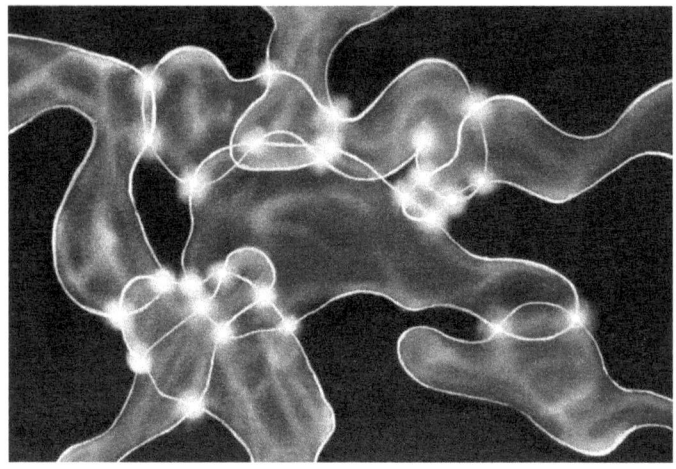

*Bubbles of Harmonies by Robert Lomax,*
*showing the points of intensity*

Let us collate and expand upon the framework I have laid out. It might become more cohesive and comprehensive for you at the same time.

Information, Pulse and Harmonies form the parts of atoms, as you have been taught. Atoms appear and disappear incredibly fast. They form from pulse in predetermined shapes which accords with the information. The information instructs or informs what should form and where. Atoms are basically energy in a program – everything is energy. Some of you talk about the holographic universe; however, that does not describe the process we have outlined. A hologram is merely pictorial information in a similar context to information fields.

Mass is a program, and the solidity of your energetic world is the resistance and interactions of its energies within particular programs. At many vibrational levels, your world is not solid. If you look at it as energy, it will become another way to interact with it. Try to imagine that you are modulating energy and all around you is a similar program. It may take quite a lot of practice or meditation to reach this stage, but it is one way for you to see objects differently at a distance and to see their inner make-up remotely. Our minds are extremely pliable in comparison to yours and we can enhance our attributes with technology to see many overlays.

If you change the information fields, you will change the resultant harmonies. For example – if one of our small craft travelled at great speed through your atmosphere, there would be problems of friction, temperature and stress. However, when we alter the 'information of the atmosphere' to not be there, it will not be created in the pulse. Literally, it doesn't exist for us. It could be said we remove the atmosphere as we approach it and reform it as we move away. But that is to see it as the relationship between two physical objects. Try to shift your mind to think about everything as 'energy and information'; perhaps temporarily forget the physical nature of our craft and imagine it as light energy.

The spacecraft of different aliens can move exceptionally fast, and at times they can appear and disappear. It's as if they have increased in velocity so significantly that their movement can't be seen with the naked eye. This is where they shift between one dimension and another, so in some ways, you are right in thinking they have disappeared, but only from one dimension to another. We do not experience excessive G-force, either, because we alter gravity and the 'moment of now' conditions. Perhaps you can begin to see how we can change some programs to suit our needs.

None of this is magic and it's not beyond your comprehension when put forward in the right way. At the moment, I am giving a basic perspective on energies and programs but will show more complexity as we move along. Hopefully, by seeing the universe in a different way, you may begin to see and appreciate yourself in a new way because you are part of it.

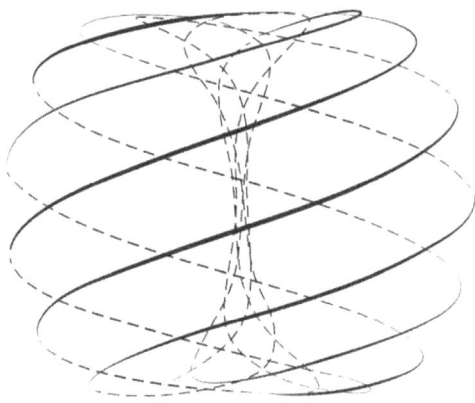

*Diagram illustrating torus energy*

I have given a few examples of energy as it appears 'to be form', but the underlying energy can also form other energies by following 'energy programs and shapes'. One example of this is where pulse energy can also present or form torus energy (folding self-perpetuating sphere). Pulse also has spiral energies either side of its formation and cessation, but I will explain those another time.

Because the pulse energy is 'on-off', it may appear as if it comes from somewhere different to this space. Pulse energy comes directly from the centre of the universe, but you will need to shift your 3d perspective – so don't over-think it.

Feel that the centre of the universe is everywhere at the same time. Feel that every part of you is the centre of the universe – that would be a new way to perceive yourself. You might like to take a moment and try this observation for yourself. Look at one of your fingers while you move it. You can see it flex fast or slowly. You are seeing what you believe is movement. It is only movement according to your perception and your beliefs. Belief, as we said earlier, is not proof. I can assure you it is **not movement** but it is an **illusion** and to help with that, we need to look at your perceptions.

You have made these movements by deliberate choice, so they cannot be devoid of consciousness. Are you more aware of body movements at slow speeds? Are they more perceivable than when typing fast? If this is the case then speed or awareness of movement is about focus or concentration within consciousness.

When typing, your focus is not on the fingers which 'seem to move' to your mental bidding. Your focus is on the words you want to type or the one beyond the next one that forms. The fingers comply with a form of consciousness program.

Your heart pumps but you don't need to focus on that program unless you wish. The brain helps with body function but it is also a tool of consciousness. Yet what credence do you give to awareness which exists within the whole body self? The very nature of your body has consciousness within it, so focus and perception are not as straightforward as it first appears. Because you continue to perceive all things at the material level, it is easy to lose sight of layers of perception and the pulse. Your fingers do not need to be your focus in order to use a keyboard with your 'typing program'. There are many consciousness programs but none of them has to be your point of focus.

The pulse need not be a part of your focus. But at its energetic level, your fingers are pulsing 'on and off'. Your fingers are being recreated constantly.

The atoms of your fingers *are here and not here* but formed in a different place. I can then say **movement does not exist** – it is all about perception – you are being recreated in a different relative position all of the time.

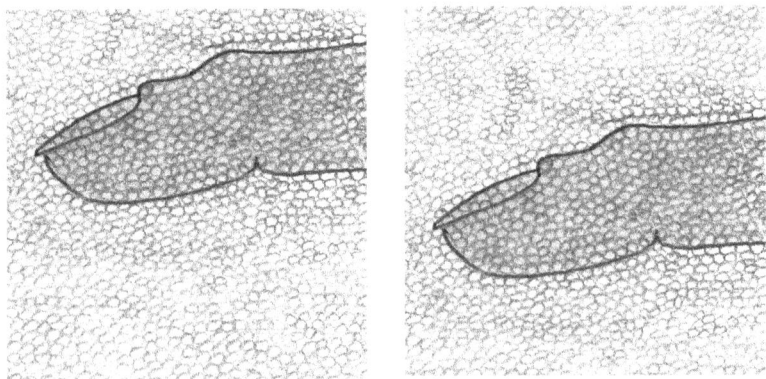

*Fingers recreated – sketched by Robert Lomax*

If you can begin to see this then I can say you are making a real difference to your perception. I did say I could assure you that movement was an illusion!

If we look at rotating earth, its orbit and spin on the edge of the Milky Way, we can begin to see that pulse in its simple complexity shows us wonder, order and inter-connectedness.

It gives us the appearance of movement and what glorious beauty it is to be part of the Isness. Every one of my words is a step, and that takes you towards a deeper appreciation of your greater energetic pliability.

As your perspective changes, it is more likely you will understand how different mine is. In this way, you may come to know me by the *WAY* in which I think. Not what I think or say. We have already challenged objectiveness as being subjective with a bias. Your bias is based upon your current ways of thinking, and I have a different bias. As you change your thinking, it will have an alternative bias.

I would like to show you different *WAYS* that you can think. This may help you create different programs for yourselves, if that's what you wish. It's not so much that you should do that but if you do not know there are alternatives, that can be rather debilitating. This is one of my primary outreach tasks, helping humans to understand our differences by understanding the *WAY* in which other humanoids think. You can only get to *know me* by stepping into my shoes and walking my footsteps. By this *'knowing'* which is also a feeling, you can be better informed to see the difference.

To be fair, you could look to see the similarities between us; perhaps expand upon soul connectedness, love and hopes. If you look at your commonality to fellow humans, this may help your society. Much of your history shows that when you looked for differences, it created divisions and conflict.

However, if you look for similarities between you and me from what you presently know, you can only see similarities that compare to your present data. That is a limited viewpoint. We have other similarities, but the details about that we have yet to impart to you because you might find them difficult to comprehend at this juncture.

The whole universe is interconnected; it lives in tandem with the inter-connectedness of soul beings. These are large topics so my presentation may vary considerably and, at times perhaps, seem random. Often, the themes may appear circular with the potential for repetitiveness. There will be no repetition – it is, by design, building layer upon layer. Knowledge can be subtle and it is not a straight line, so neither is the gaining of it.

You may wish to grasp for knowledge, but what would you take hold of first? If you are to receive a new gift of knowledge, but your hands are full, it would mean that you would need to put down and let go of that which you hold dear to yourself. Your ideas are important to you – otherwise, you would not be holding them. How would you understand new knowledge? Through what level of a database – what blinkers – what bias?

You have your ideas of freedom and we certainly do not judge. So, if you wish to gain knowledge by grabbing the first thing that comes to mind, then do so. That is one definition of freedom within your program and if you wish, exercise it.

When you express desire, you are using it to form your actions but not always what you initially wished for. In this instance above, the desire to assimilate knowledge in any order would require you to face 'why you grasp from where you are lacking'. If you found an enlightened aspect of information which said 'nothing really moves', it would make no sense unless you had sufficient context.

Now that you have the context, it is not nonsense. So the order is helpful, and as a guide also for Robert, I know how best to advance his understanding. As your guides will for you.

Advancing or bringing forward knowledge is not always about

hard work or a wish to know more. There are ways of thinking that do not require a desire to drive you forwards – where a database is not needed to understand or know. This is all very different from the way you think.

These are quite some claims, and among others yet to come. So who am I that I should say such things with certainty and candour? To dare to say, "I know what you are by the WAY that you think."

One simple explanation is that I am a version of you – a version of soul. I claim to be no more than that – a servant of myself.

## The way that you think in duality

In order to know the *WAY*, I think it is incumbent upon you to know the *WAY* you think. You think you know what you think, but do you really know the *WAY* that you do it?

You have many good psychologists who will recognise much of what I say but take issue with other aspects of my presentation. In part, that might be because I am talking about this on energetic levels. For some of you this may feel somewhat trite, but for a few these are new or unknown mental constructs. I do not intend to leave the few behind.

I have lived long, studied and lectured much. I have access to ancillary wisdom and different ways of accessing it than you do. I do not propose to hold back, and I will say it as it is – as we Andromedans see it. Your phrase is 'to drive the nail hard'. If you are offended by what I say or the way I say it, I could apologise, but I would only be doing so to assuage your feelings – and that would be rather pointless. Is it not the sign of true friendship to give with honesty and love? Though already we have hit a hurdle because we have different definitions of love.

Your program is akin to walking into a hallway of mirrors – warped, bent, broken or dulled. When you look at your reflection, it is distorted. You believe it is true because you have no other information to the contrary. The program keeps you in the program. That is its design until you decide otherwise. This insidious program works through your counterpart lives in the subconscious.

(That last sentence will require context to fully understand it.) I will use your term 'subconscious' as the description of your default or mainframe running program. It is your way of being, despite what you sometimes wish. You already know many parts of your subconscious programs.

The things and ideas that you are not aware of, I will refer to with the use of your term 'unconscious'. These are the things that you are not aware of at your current level of focus. You are also unconscious of parts of your subconscious program. In other words, you won't know all your subconscious programs. Your awareness also depends upon your levels of focus and what you believe you are conscious of.

Counterpart lives within the subconscious programs are the freewill accorded to your thoughts and feelings. These can believe they are separate in the same way you believe you are separate and individual in the universe. They have the autonomy to create constructs and coping strategies, which in turn affect you because they are you – though you may be unconscious of them.

We have already used the terms collective consciousness, universal and higher consciousness. While I have been talking, you have probably realised that your idea of 'free will' is being challenged. I spoke of the program to keep you in the program. I talked about the connectedness of all things. So if you are connected to all things then you cannot be free of them. I would say, "I am free from thinking *that I am not free.*" It is not on my radar because it has no meaning or relevance to my life. There are other ways to think about this including *freedom doesn't exist.* In which case, I would say freedom is a restrictive concept and only exists by virtue of and for those that seek it.

This is not easy to understand and sounds as if it is double speak or nonsense, but it's worthwhile spending some time on it. Duality is a huge stumbling block to humanity and it means you are not free from some of the programs of the collective and subconscious. The thought of moving from your current program may seem a little daunting, however, it is only a 'different way of thinking'. It will only become a different way of being if you choose another method for processing. How could you know that there are different *WAYS* of thinking when the existing ways hold you tightly in their program? All this because it fits your definition of life, therefore it seems the only way. As to your freedom, what is that within a jail of your own construct? You cannot easily see the way out, as it is also hampered by separation and counterpart lives.

Some of you will think freedom, free will and autonomy must exist; they are the counterparts and regulators of bullies, financiers and oppressors. Of course, oppression should not be accepted – assuming there is agreement upon what it is or where you see it. Many wars are fought in the name of freedom, only to have alternative oppression rolled out by the leaders of the victors. A 'revolution' is to go round and round. Evolution is to evolve and if you want that there is no better place to start than in the heart and your subconscious. 'True freedom from oppression' *is not needing freedom from oppression* – freedom from oppressors need not then exist. You might think that is not possible, but it is. It is the way we live in harmony and love.

25

Freedom and free will can also be illusive, particularly if they come at the price of compromise. When do your free will and desire become an imposition upon another person? If they acquiesce to you because of a distorted fear program in their subconscious, does it mean you have taken advantage of them? If your subconscious is clear of any negativity and you are able to see their default programs then the answer could be yes. Though only you can be the judge of yourself, and if your subconscious were that clear then your current earth life would be out of kilter to the rest.

As Andromedans, if we were to take advantage of other gentle souls, it would cause us emotional and physical pain because we would be taking advantage of ourselves (in the wider sense).

So, can you be an oppressor or dictator? In denial or gentleness, you might like to think not, but you do control your feelings and thoughts.

Feelings have their own need to be free from oppression. It may help to look upon these counterpart lives in much the same way, as we are a counterpart life of our higher multidimensional selves. They have responsibility and love for us in a similar way that we should have for our feelings and thoughts.

How you treat feelings in your subconscious creates adaptations to your *run program*. What you exercise internally becomes your external expression. Then the outside world reflects back to you your initial or sponsoring thoughts. What you see on the outside is yourself. The universe does this because it is an extension of you and you of it. You feel, think, act and that is one of the processes of creation.

No doubt you have heard concepts like this before, but have you ever really considered that your thoughts and feelings have self-awareness? That they are autonomous within you? One of your sayings is 'freedom is a god-given right'. If that is so then it should be that way for 'every part of you', otherwise it is restricted or partial. That is difficult for some of you because you do not trust your own selves as individuals.

Freedom can come in many forms and you may choose to use 'the freedom to be an oppressor'. It is a widely held view that you need to be master over your feelings. Being in control doesn't seem wrong; you certainly wouldn't want to be out of control or for feelings to dictate to you. Because you control yourself in order to be who you want, then a part of you becomes dictated to.

You are both the dictator and the dictated.

It may be easier to grasp this by reminding yourself of the earlier statement 'that all is energy'. That includes thoughts and emotions, some of which you keep at arm's length. Your desire to be an individual with self-autonomy is blended with many other feelings and thoughts in the subconscious. These thoughts and feelings are only partially known to other thoughts and feelings, and often you are unconscious of them (not fully conscious). Sometimes you do not know the true feel of a feeling, which I will cover in a moment.

The reasons for partially known thoughts may include the following: a lack of evolution or enlightenment; a desire to escape self-responsibility (usually hidden under the veil of freedom when in fact it is a way of removing yourself from pain or difficulty); a singular or one-sided outlook on multifaceted situations.

Imagine yourself as an entity completely aware of all aspects of yourself, but your wisdom is limited to your present knowledge. You are the self and 'all of you' is your domain. Bring to your mind a planet floating in space with its own orbiting debris field. The planet would be a metaphor for your head, encircled by rocks, which are thoughts and emotions.

Every rock is its *'own self'*; it is an individual as it bumps and crashes around. Yet each of them is a part of you, but you only know them as they know themselves in their limited experience. Their experience is hampered by separation and autonomy from the whole self (the planet plus the rest of the debris field). This all exists within an area of space that contains duality programming.

You will know the following examples well in their singularity or opposition.

- *I want to be happy.*
- *I want to be loved more.*
- *I like being helped and encouraged.*
- *I want to have these feelings as much as is possible.*

Like the bumping rocks, the feelings in the debris field or subconscious can link themselves to each other because of a past experience. For example, *'Being helped means I am loved and that makes me happy'*. But in singularity and autonomy, these feelings are not often aware of the opposite or alternative perception – the one that exists in duality or paradox.

If you *'want to be happy'* that must come from the perspective that you are not – otherwise, you would be happy and you would not desire it. The same applies to the other examples given. In order to be loved more, it means you are not loved enough. To desire help is to be in a position where you need to be helped or made to feel better. All these positive desire feelings have a counterpart within paradox or duality. The last one being *'to have these feelings as much as possible'* shows you do not know what you are wishing for.

Do the positive desires know that they have a counterpart,

which is as much a part of them as they are of it; do they know that they are you and you are them? One cannot exist without the other. Showing you the planet and rock field gives ownership of feelings and thoughts – it is a part of your program and you are also it. You are every one of these separate autonomous rocks. You are the complete system. However, accepting it in this way does raise a few questions.

If you do not choose happiness, is there 'no happiness'? That, however, is the illusion of choice (something we will cover). It is duality running rampant in your subconscious and it is a life in paradox. It's just as impossible to grasp water from a running tap.

Do you believe that you think differently to this?

Would it be good to wish you were strong and brave – perhaps brave in every moment? Yet in order to be brave, you must be afraid. If you were not afraid you could not be brave. Bravery does not exist without fear – this *way* of thinking means you create fear constantly with the wish to be brave in every moment. Remember it is you that creates but often have little idea of what you create.

Words can be used flippantly – for example, 'anxious'. Somehow it's more acceptable to use that word than 'fear'. A little anxious – a measurement – as if you should welcome or be pleased that it is only small. Do not fear to say fear. Nor find that being a little anxious is acceptable.

As well as a predisposition to grasp for positive ideals, you can do the same with negative thoughts. Many hold on to fear as a form of protection – that is bizarre, isn't it? But it's true.

Imagine you live a reasonable life and manage with a few mental conflicts or a little anxiety. That's what life is – isn't it? It's always been the same. Stick to the status quo, it's easy, why change thoughts? It could be worse (there we have negative thought used as a form of comfort). So, if there is no demonstrable harm or threat, why move from where you are? You have all you need within your current mental boundaries. These can be high stonewalls that form protection, safety in mild suffering. But there is always a way out of such a thought trap, for in one corner exists a locked door. You have always had the key in your pocket; you are after all the key to your own mind. Beyond the walls, all manner of wonderful or terrible things could exist. Surely fear doesn't rule all things? What harm can it do to take a peek in the subconscious — what will it say?

*It might be dangerous; you might be given a temptation you cannot resist — you might forget who you are and where you came from, then you would be lost. If you do not have your fear of the unknown, your innocence will be your undoing.*

So hold tightly to fear as it keeps you safe, and if we follow this in duality it ultimately leads to, *'I fear the loss of my fear.'* You may not be conscious of it as a program but it is a thought trap, which is difficult to escape.

Upon reflection, you can see you are safe in your fears as well as unsafe; they co-exist side by side as a paradox that has no solution. There are many thoughts in the collective that are passed among you. Often they are seen as motivational: *'to aspire to be better is a good thing'*. Hold a yardstick (measuring stick) next to you; make sure it is one inch taller than you are, then you will always have something to aspire to. But, consequently, you will always feel you are never good enough.

Lack of enlightenment is prevalent in all such thoughts, yet you allow these to run your subconscious programs! How often do you think you are feeling the pertinent feeling for a particular experience? All the time is probably the answer. But you often feel one feeling through another one.

During loss or bereavement, feelings can surge up and down like a roller coaster. Sadness is not welcomed by anyone, particularly when it flows back with full force after a respite. Because the subconscious can experience counterpart lives, many rocks in the debris field can be either afraid generally or specifically of sadness. Very few people welcome sadness and not wanting its return means you have a 'fear of sadness' – that is to feel sadness through fear. Sadness by itself is just sad; it is nothing to be afraid of. The more you allow yourself into the sadness without resistance, the less it becomes a bush of emotional thorns.

You often feel one feeling through another without knowing that you do, and these feelings can arise as if from nowhere – not relevant to your current situation. This can cause great confusion – sometimes there is a sense of 'unknown feelings', which in turn create more worry. Not only can feelings become attached to each other but also experiences and vice versa. These also inform your subconscious programs.

If you were rebuked or told off when you were a child, that's a perfectly normal thing. Privileges might be withdrawn and the verbal chastisement will cause emotional pain. How would this event impact upon your subconscious if you had done nothing wrong and, despite protestations, you were not believed? You had no ability or power to change the situation, all because you had done nothing wrong. You would likely become angry and wounded banished to your room to brood and suffer in silence to stay there until you are able to say sorry. Life is so unfair and so unjust. If there is no reason for life to be so cruel, perhaps it has no meaning.

These beliefs will form deep grooves in a vinyl record, and the more the record is played the deeper the grooves will become until the needle has no way out. The feelings become attached to one another and are reinforced by other events as life goes on. But you are older now; you know yourself and you are wiser. You cut your foot on the broken glass that you did not clear away yesterday. You feel pain – you are angry with yourself – yet somewhere there is a feeling that it's *unfair, not your fault.* When fairness or deserving is irrelevant, *you feel you are being punished* for a mistake, not an intention. But punishment has no part of the situation – it is cause and effect. Yet the *pain feels like punishment.*

You *need to feel better* – so seek reassurance and love from another. Even if they give comfort, it doesn't really heal these disparate feelings that course around you. They are your feelings and cannot be taken away by someone else. But at least you can let them know of your pain.

The loving sympathiser turns the tables, "It's your own fault, you should have cleared it away yesterday." But you forgot to because you were distracted by helping the potential sympathiser and if you respond to that it will cause an argument – *so best keep quiet and suffer in silence even if it's your fault – this is so unfair.*

You will be amazed at what feelings can become attached to a particular event. It works the other way round as well. If you feel an injustice as an adult, your mind can be transported back to the suffering and ruminations in the childhood bedroom. Old events often pop into the mind as if from nowhere. Until you work through the attachments, that is.

Duality and paradox can create some unusual effects in the subconscious. You are both the programmer and the program. The program works instantaneously – there is no delay – all your thoughts and possibilities are instantly accessed. Often the program is on 'repeat run' as if it controls you. We see this 'play auto' response when people become angry or aggressive. Such people are afraid – they do not want arguments or confrontation so they choose weak people to have in their lives. By creating a prickly and aggressive persona, those lacking in confidence acquiesce to their demands. However, using such programs with others who are not weak causes arguments and confrontation. Then they have created the very thing they wished to avoid – they face their fear, the very thing that can help them change and grow.

Paradox extends its tentacles into depression, which might be viewed as the inability to feel better or get better. *There is no answer/no solution* is a depressing feeling but few see the depth of the conundrum. Paradox has no answer – that is the nature of a paradox and duality. Some people do not wish to get better.

- *When I try to get better it always fails – at some stage, I always return to this low point.*
- *There is no point in trying – when I do get better, I fall back and I feel worse again.*
- *There is nothing worse than things getting worse – so if things can't get any worse that is a good thing – that is safety!*
- *If I stay at the bottom of my pit in the deepest darkest crevice, I can live in my suffering but at least here it can't get any worse.*
- *Let me seek and live in the worst of the worst.*

While this seems crazy, these feelings are perfectly logical and, at their level of individuality and counterpart awareness, they make sense in the subconscious. You can only see the rationale is one side of a duality program when it comes out into the conscious awareness. These mini aspects of you have free will to think and feel. Your feelings create programs but they are not fully conscious nor are you fully conscious of them till you are.

A process of counselling, education or enlightenment can bring them into the light. Often people talk of hurts or problems and that helps. But do not leave the issues as exposed washing, flapping and making a noise on the drying line. To talk without reaching an understanding of the depth of the **'causes in duality'** is to fall short of reprogramming the mind. Actions and deeds do turn negative situations around, but understanding and healing within duality are not only enlightening, but they also change the *way* you think. If only you could see what difference these changes make to your energy, perhaps then you would wish to know yourself more fully.

How do you escape duality's opposing thoughts in a paradox? The answer is simple – you don't; that's the answer in a paradox – you don't do anything! This is very different to a therapist saying "it's about letting go" – it's about not energising it to then have to let it go. It's about not having it in your choices or on your radar because it's not split in duality. In this way, you do not even need to walk the middle path between opposing desires or thoughts. Otherwise, that's still having them and trying to keep some kind of equilibrium.

For equilibrium, imagine a seesaw where you can place variable weights at different distances on a beam either side of a central pivot. It is a duality balance in the subconscious, which can be maintained and weighted accordingly. It holds many complex thoughts and issues (providing the beam is strong enough). But one small challenging experience could put things out of kilter.

As the seesaw beam begins to tilt in one direction, all the weights on both sides will start to slide and could cause a major imbalance. That requires quick reactions to reverse the situation. In haste it is easy to over-compensate, causing the beam to veer from the initial tilt to the opposite one. We could use your term 'bi-polar' for this action.

So what can be done with all these weights needing to be balanced? I did say do nothing with paradox. That was in relation to not needing the weights, not energising the potential. After 'clearing or enlightening' your unknown thoughts that corrupt the subconscious, you will need nothing. There will be no need to maintain a balance – there will be nothing to balance; there will be no thoughts that oppose themselves and no seesaw. Imagine how much extra energy you will have when you have dispensed with this way of thinking.

If you believe you are free of duality, I would say you are not prepared to accept the understanding of who you are. Oh, I can hear challenges such as, "I am here to move earth forward and to change the electromagnetic vibration of my family's DNA and karma." Yes, but that is through doing the work that I have outlined above. Many ignore or turn away from such tasks – fearing them or believing they are too difficult.

So, no weights to balance and no beam to hold them, or certainly a less complicated system of weights, while you continue to work on it. Just because paradox exists doesn't mean you have to keep trying to solve the unsolvable. That's distraction solving to give greater value to something else in order to avoid a particularly difficult issue. Most of the time you will not see the avoidance only hard work and pressures elsewhere. Your mind has an incalculable arsenal of opposing thoughts in duality. But if you need a few more, don't forget you are plugged into the collective consciousness of your planet – you are a part of everything.

That brings in an interesting observation. The thoughts you think now – are they yours or the collective? Have they been thought before? Is there new thought or just different ways of doing the same things in a different context?

I could have started this part of my dialogue by saying, "Is there any such thing as original thought?" Like earlier comments this challenges concepts of self, separateness and individuality. If you find a new unconscious thought, did you discover it? Because even if you found it within you or the universal consciousness, it existed before you found it. Does invention exist without pre-thought; if so what is pre-thought? The answers to these are another way to unravel individuality and head towards the connectedness of all.

The question of invention needs to be seen in its relationship to – multidimensionality and non-time as well as *creating anew,* which will be talked about later. There are different answers on different dimensions to these thoughts. It is also paradoxical – how can it exist if it doesn't exist? The answer is also yes and no at the same time, and it will challenge thought boundaries and current concepts.

Of course, there is 'individual expression and experience'; you think you experience that but, nonetheless, the basic building blocks of the human way of thinking still exist.

They can be divided or chopped up; they can be multiplied and clumped together in different concepts. But when you look into a complex thought process you will still see the interaction of individuation and the feelings based in duality.

Your personal individuality is your expression it is not the same thing as '*the way of processing possibilities*'. Humanity has many creative and artistic people in all areas of life. So how do you experience inspiration – the 'aha moment' when perhaps a missing link has been found? Years of hard work lead to one moment of inspiration. A musician might wake in the morning with a fully formed tune in their head. Did that just happen or have they just remembered what they did in their sleep and if so, were their multidimensional selves involved? Was it a program that runs till algorithms form and creates a melody? It may have happened as if in a moment, but that was just the awareness of it presented in your daily consciousness. And all this happened in the 'moment of now' without time being involved!

I have posed many questions so when is a question an answer? Providing unusual answers or more questions to paradoxical questions may perplex you. In order to see a greater fullness within my words, you will need to have a good understanding of *'several different ways of thinking'*.

If you changed your ways of thinking, you would have greater mental pliability. You would be able to see from unfixed and non-linear points of focus. At the moment, you see through your current beliefs but you might loosen your grip on them if you are shown other ways.

To help, I will talk about other beings and 'their way of processing', then later you will see us take Robert to visit entities he has not previously encountered, where again completely different ways of thinking will be shown.

## Other ways of thinking and being

Aside from the differences in my body compounds, I do not think like you nor do I act from the same stimuli. My life is not less interesting or more interesting than yours. Is it more fulfilling? That depends on what you regard as fulfilling, we would have very different ideas on that. One of your biggest hurdles is that you measure things and make judgements in relativity.

I do not compare and value things in the ways that you do, I function perfectly well without. Note that I have not said this makes me happier or better than you – that would be a comparison. I exist and live without judgements. I am using your words 'comparison and judgement' to convey my meaning, so I need to make sure my use of them is the same as yours.

**Comparisons:** Measuring things that are relevant to you in ways they relate to you, which exist as programs in the subconscious. A bully in the playground sees someone feeling better than they do, so they see their own unhappiness in greater in starkness. Logic says if someone else feels worse than you then you must be feeling better than them. A simple case of comparing emotions relative to one another and the rationale for making someone else cry is formed. Having long passed through the playground, you all know someone else's unhappiness doesn't make you internally happy, but it does show how comparisons can be distorted while using them in duality.

**Judgement:** Right and wrong – *I feel bad therefore I am bad, so I might as well be bad and carry on doing the same thing.* Sooner or later in life, that rope gets pulled in all the way, only to find there is nothing on the end of it! The essence of good or bad often revolves around thinking you are not good enough or that being punished puts things right.

Good or bad does not exist for me. That is a form of measurement that excludes love and understanding. Mistakes are made by everyone – that is the ability to look back at what you have done and say I could have done that differently. It is not a matter that you could have done it better – better is a value and connects with good or bad.

Feeling and believing you are what you feel creates a further detachment from the reality of a situation. If you held a bag of ice in your hand, you would experience cold – you sense or detect it. You don't say I'm feeling cold therefore I am cold when it's only affecting your hand. You can feel anger but you have the choice to be angry or not. This is not about the suppression of feelings. If your choice is based in wisdom and balance you won't have subconscious emotions that override decisions. You can still have the feelings if you wish, but they can become enlightened and a trusted part of your psyche in harmony with you.

Your body make-up is different to mine – your hormones, electrical and chemical processes also reflect in your body what you feel. In return, they give you the bodily experience and this feeds back to you. If you are not based in love, this can be an explosive experience. We experience some negative emotions but they do not have the same effect nor do we need to act upon them. This does not mean we are dull or bland or that we cannot act in any way we wish.

We have personality and individuality; we all express ourselves to the mental and emotional programs that we chose. The use of the word *programs* may sound rather mechanical and I could have used your word, subconscious – but to us, it is not an 'unknown domain' being sub or below our conscious. For us, it is more integrated. We don't need to control the way we function because we are more harmonious. That is why I used the word *program* to show our differences. I could have used the term 'control over' to show the difference between us, where you are not in full control or at times out of control. Our subconscious has been programmed so that it is not unknown, and it fully enters our conscious harmony. From such ways of being, we create our way of living and loving.

I have been careful in describing the 'way' we view you and your 'ways'. We can see that there are several self-awareness issues that impair the human's ability to be the best expression of themselves. This lack of self-awareness is like living under veils of cloth – it limits your perception of finer vibrations and higher functioning souls. This is not an insult because even the *'Robert me'* does not function as this me.

## Different ways

You have such great potential in so many areas but you are what you believe you are – till you are not. By that I mean you can be like other beings who have exceeded the need to *let go of mental constraints* – they just don't have them. You could be like other beings and *exceed your own beliefs in who you are* because beliefs are limiting.

'Non-locality perspective' A phrase I have not defined. Sounds interesting but does it have relevance to your perspective? Let us see in a while.

There are connections between your different levels of consciousness, but many of these you are unaware of. You work from your database constrained by what you know. It's like carrying heavy stepping-stones just in case you encounter a stream in a desert.

You might not agree with that and think your *'way'* seems to work perfectly well. That understanding or learning grows from your foundations and one thing builds upon another. However, that depends upon the material you use for the foundations. If the material is anything like your subconscious, you might think again. I might appear to be working from foundations with my explanations, but I am using overlays.

Your way of growing is to use your evolving database as a stepping-stone to promote your next move or direction. I am providing dimensional layers and interconnected matters – a bit like looking at plans of different levels in the same place.

You can only create or think of things based upon current beliefs and knowledge because you work from what you already know. The foundations you have will only get you so far. I am not saying your way is wrong – there is no judgement here.

## Different feelings

Andromedans are part of a loving collective where there are no lies and no reasons to lie. No fragile egos or loss of face but unfettered interaction without judgement. We do not seek betterment over one another; we love each other as we would ourselves, in fullness. This is a joyous feeling; it is a heightened spiritual life and not an ecstasy removed from reality. Perhaps it would be useful if the Robert 'me' can impart what our society feels like from the human perspective rather than my Andromedan bias.

**Robert (R):** When I am in close proximity or viewing their living world, it feels like I am entering a utopian realm. I am aware that my understanding of utopia is my perspective and for them, it would not compute. Utopia would be a comparison and value.

I know their world can change if it needs to adapt, even though it seems to be a wonderful expression already. The contrast between our worlds is difficult to describe. I don't have to 'try at doing anything' nor look at myself as I do on earth. Achievement or measurement of self does not exist in the collective consciousness; it is just not relevant. It feels that the burdens we all individually carry have evaporated without deciding to dispense with them. I know that I know their places, people and information, but I can't always access those memories. Either the processor isn't there to connect to or this level of my consciousness is incapable.

Being welcomed is an understatement for what I feel and my words seem to fall short; we need a new vocabulary. It's a place of unconditional love. I feel as if everybody loves me as their prime process and without any question as to my inadequacies or lower vibrations. There is a sense of oneness and connection with all things – even the plants and animals feel as if they are extensions of me. Some of the plants make vibrations you can hear or sense and they respond to my thoughts. Everything is so interconnected that you can see instant energetic reactions to what is said or done. At times, my earthly thoughts seem incongruous and out of place. My earth mind seems so shallow and some of my thoughts have no relevance. There is great intelligence but all of that seems to be an extension of spirituality. It feels like home but it's much more than that – it's like I already belong there and I am only here on earth for a short visit despite the previous lives I've had. The thought of returning to my earth consciousness sometimes fills me with a tinge of sadness.

Being with the Andromedans is not a sweet and fluffy automatism to pre-set programmed ways of living. Far from it, there are many cutting edge conversations (well for me). Love here is forthright, honest and challenging because it 'just is' and that's so refreshing. That has helped me see myself in different ways, though some interactions can be quite humorous.

For one of my first Andromedan mental trips, Antemedi took me to a female who was just 'sightseeing'; she was on vacation observing humanity out of interest. Well, why not, I thought! She showed me her mental enhancement devices, explaining that she could locate souls of a different frequency with specific signatures and inter-connectedness. My music was playing in the background and I asked her what she thought of it. She said, "You are all so creative but your music and the lyrics are so sad. In some ways, you see love so differently to us. At times you wallow in sadness; you see escaping from sadness as a form of release – as if it is a joy to escape turmoil and heartache. To us this is not joy nor love of the self, this is just escaping from pain. Why not live in the fullness of love then you will not have to seek it?"

I could see the sense in that and it made me realise how limited our lives are. She explained that her music was based around harmonics of higher feelings, vibrational tones and universe resonances. I tried to hear what she projected but I could not attune to it.

Talking of love reminds me of the time I was taken to an educational exchange. I was asked to give my human definition to those present in one of the rooms of the 'multifunctional building'.

You know all the usual definitions of love without my need to repeat them. A few of the participants were, however, absolutely shocked to hear me say that some humans also 'trade love' like a commodity.

They value it depending on the reason it's given or the esteem in which they hold the person who gives it. Often it's given in anticipation that it should be returned. If it doesn't come back in the way or the amount wanted, we could withdraw our love to punish or show we are wounded.

All this is to get what we want, which is to make us feel loved and appreciated. A couple of the participants could not comprehend this and had difficulty processing it because it felt energetically dark and alien to their way of thinking. It was

*The multifunctional building, as painted by Robert Lomax*

certainly not their experience of love. I try to be respectful of others but on one occasion my human feelings caused me great embarrassment.

I met a female Andromedan called Argoney after she had finished a lecture. To say she was spellbinding does not do her justice. She was so attractive on so many levels but it was her energetic resonance that was so captivating. I tried not to look at her face or engage with her eyes – what I was feeling was so inappropriate and so strong. She was very tactful and gentle and tried to make light of the situation, obviously knowing what was going on for me.

She explained that it was perfectly normal for lower light frequency individuals to be drawn to higher frequency male or female beings who emit unconditional love. Add to that mix our human endorphins and electro/chemical systems (mentioned earlier) and there was quite an overload. They are fully aware this could be an issue during any encounters between the races and sexes. Though they do have technology that can project mental and emotional programs to overcome that. She talked about my misconceptions of society values and was happy to show me two children playing with vibrational jigsaw pieces. It was a toy designed to help them *think and see in vibrational harmonies;* in that way, it would become a *knowing* and one of their ways of being.

'Communing' is yet another type of feeling. I was walked up on to the sloped roof of the multifunctional building. The access ramps to this area slide out from the edge of the fascia (left-hand side of painting). The roof then reaches down to the external ground floor. There are also lifts and steps within the main foyer that go up to the roof. Automatic foldaway covers open to reveal very comfortable seating.

As in the lecture and meeting rooms, the chairs contain several technical devices including holographic projectors. They are quite intense and you feel you are able to lose yourself inside them, to actually be where you are looking, though they can be used for diagrams and other information.

However, they were not needed, and when we were all settled, the chairs reclined so that our heads pointed towards the highest edge of the roof. It wasn't a joint meditation it was a meeting by union with everyone else's energy. I was a part of everyone else who was there. I had never felt anything like that before. Waves of energies rolled from side to side, sometimes unfolding in the heart. It was soporific and joyous with no loss of consciousness.

Apparently, in some events, they concentrate and project love energies to help specific universal developments – though technology can be used to enhance projections. After the event, there was an orderly exit and I was taken down steps through the main foyer or lobby to several levels below. We came to a transportation hub of 'floating plates' with handrails. Antemedi showed me how to place our hands on the rail. An energetic bubble of some kind surrounded both the plate and us. It took off, swiftly moving from one tube to another without the feeling of acceleration or turning. It interacted with his thoughts and arrived where he desired to be.

There are a wide variety of experiences as well as feelings that are different to everyday human ones. Resonance chambers fall into this category and are quite extraordinary when used for energetic healing. Negative thought patterns can be discharged or removed so that new or alternative energies can be inserted.

These contain information including thoughts and emotions. I could 'feel' the sound of these intensities and occasionally there would be dragging or drawing sensations from certain parts of my body, usually tickly or just weird. The incoming energies often felt like pinpricks or dull pains. Nothing very uncomfortable, quite exciting as it usually meant some new thought concepts to look at when the energy had settled. I hasten to add that this process is nothing like other alien abductions and experimentation.

Another uplifting feeling for me is the energetic body merging. This doesn't have to be technology-based. It's not frightening but as you feel yourself in a different body shape it makes you realise everything is just a matter of perception and energy. It's all very gentle and done with permission.

It's happened several times, either to broaden my feelings or as a form of education. Twice I have met with an amphibian Cytith called Trito. I was able to enter an energy 'over-form' and have an incredible experience swimming in water with huge arms and legs. The breathing was different and he seemed to have gills as well as the ability to breathe air. I had an awareness of a big lung capacity that could be squeezed by strong ribs to reduce buoyancy and change depths. Coming back on to a rocky shore was easy using dextrous gripper pads and retractable talons in the palms.

The fingers, however, were very dextrous and delicate – rather at odds with his overall appearance. He had great humility and a deep wide feeling of natural pride that didn't seem unbalanced in his stature. I was quite taken by those two encounters so I recorded them at the time. (See References for links to [3]*Cytith Aquatic Humanoid* and [4]*Second Meeting Cytith*.)

Another merge was with Telenatey, an Andromedan botanist working with plant energies. It was extraordinary the way plants were able to interact through some form of energetic consciousness. One old tree, in particular, had no more room for root growth next to buildings and had decided to throw out new suckers for the first time in order that it could die to feed its offspring.

Telenatey showed me how they create new plant variations using 'objective information' as a vibrational program. Sort of jumping forward in evolution using the energy information of a new environment to adapt or create a plant. The information of the plant could 'form' to suit the circumstances. This meant they could help vegetation to recover or adapt to new environments. He showed how they used consciousness programs to see the outcomes of plant interactions with existing vegetation or reproduction cycles of new plants.

I have more to say but, hopefully, that's sufficient to show my personal human perception.

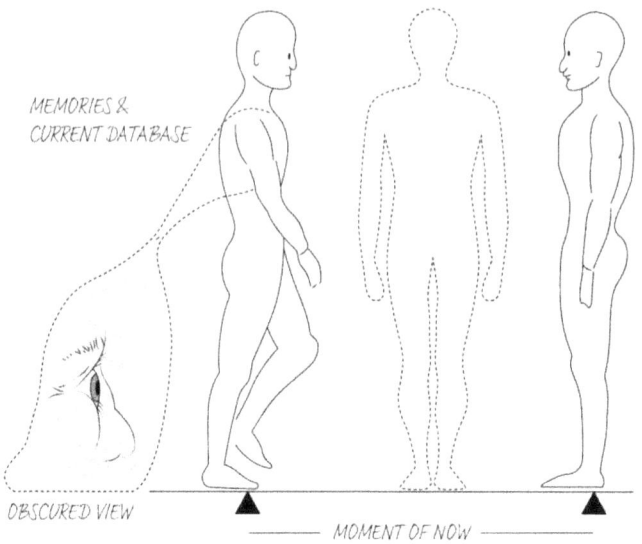

MEMORIES &
CURRENT DATABASE

OBSCURED VIEW

MOMENT OF NOW

*The Moment of Now diagram shown by Antemedi*

**Antemedi (A):** Your description is a little more effervescent than we would have used. Our vibrations are finer, which means there is a greater contrast; this is what you felt and commented on.

I have given my perspective on how we are not like you but only a glimpse of the 'way' we think. So at this juncture, it would be useful to look at other *'ways'* of thinking.

The figure on the left represents you and your human method of looking forwards. You have a bag of data and a program system to make comparisons and measurements. This is projected into the future to see or create new possibilities; always planning and preparing for the next moment and for what is wanted or not.

The three figures together represent the moment of now. On

the left, *past now* is looking forward with past data towards the central moment of now figure. The figure on the right is the *future now,* looking back towards the central *moment of now* figure. The moment of now contains all three figures and has been drawn to conceptualise different perspectives or ways of thinking.

I think it will be useful to look at one of your old thought puzzles, which asks, "How long is the moment of now?" If you were able to measure it, would it be one second, a millionth of a second or even smaller than that?

Are you thinking in the now or are you just catching up with your thoughts from before? You view the moment of now in a human perception within a linear dimension.

Some think the moment of now exists in between the past and the future because they feel they can't exist in the past or the future, but that is not the case. As soon as the past is finished the future starts. There is no time or space between the past now and the future now you can't even get a thought concept between them, let alone a piece of paper. In order to exist, you must be in both. You have a foot in each camp and you straddle time, existing in both the future and the past. You can put your awareness into any aspect of the moment of now, but remember you exist in non-space and are multidimensional; but that's a different topic to 'ways of thinking'.

For a moment, let us put aside 'pulse' and 'no movement'. The figure in the middle represents a span of consciousness in the moment of now with feet either side of the pivot in past and future. The other two figures represent ways of thinking.

Memory is a way of recalling an event. Humans tend to see the past as fixed or gone and that's a description of history, whereas life itself is an experience that is happening or about to happen. It's all about what is coming, and this is what gives you the feeling of being able to create and experience what you plan for.

The future is observed by looking towards it. By looking towards it you automatically place your focus or vantage point in the 'past moment of now'. But you are only seeing possibilities from your current fixed perspective. In this way, you limit the 'future you' and your possibilities to the definitions in your current perspective within the 'past moment of now'. You create from what you are, and what you create is a replication or a mirror of your fixed position; it is a form of blindness. I hope this shows you that the Andromedan observations I made earlier were from a more fluid position.

Andromedans can allow themselves to be in *the moment of now* in a similar way to you, but we can also turn our focus backwards in order to see our way forward.

When humans look back, you look at history from the position on the left of the diagram. If we place our focus on the right-hand figure of the diagram, we can look to the left, back over *the moment of now* from 'forward focus in *the moment of now*'.

(Note: it is also possible to look forwards from the *forward now* right-hand position; this is to look at the unlimited from the unlimited – that is different again)

If we had a problem to solve we would believe that we had found the solution or were living it. We would be in the 'knowing' or 'just is' without constraints. We look back at what enabled us to be where we are (in the future if you like) and retrace the formative route.

In your human experience, if you imagine or wish to create something, you hold it in your mind. You can look at the steps you need to take to get there, but what you create is still bounded by your point of focus and your knowledge. Nothing wrong with that, it serves many humanoids – including us – well. However, we have more data and enhanced ways of accessing it. We are not bound by duality or corrupted subconscious programs. We are less attached and not formulaic so we experience your way of thinking at another level.

If you have no specific desires for an outcome, it is easier to take yourself forward with love and openness. In this way, you do not distort or influence what you see. The options that come to you from alignment with the Isness are far greater than you could imagine. You will not be overloaded with information and there is no need to filter because that would inhibit.

Looking back as a way of looking forwards sounds counter-intuitive. All of this comes through trusting higher self and the universe, which is you. This way of thinking is as natural as breathing the next breath. It means we are 'open to the desires of others' which has great harmonious possibilities. As individuals, we would not put ourselves into a freethinking position only to limit it by a personal desire. These harmonious possibilities might seem like a loss of self -interest but that's not how we think.

From an open perspective, we can also see the likely outcome of events and what we are to encounter, provided (that's a big proviso) we don't alter actions or events significantly. If we choose to live in that mode, we need to be very loving and very much attuned to the Isness.

If you become aware of a future event that would have a significant personal impact, you would have difficulty coping with the duality emotions and seesaw subconscious programs.

For those that can and choose to live this way, it adds another dimension.

Humanity and some other races tend to live in the immediacy of the now moment. You create cause and effect and experience it for the first time without pre-knowledge. There are more programs involved with pre-knowledge but you don't experience it that way. It all appears fresh and not pre-programmed as if you are in charge of yourself within the moment. It is one of the attributes of your dimension. You do not consciously use the union of the multidimensional self, nor are you really aware that this union can actually exist.

Many of my experiences have been from the perspective that you inhabit, but I do not need to live that unless I wish. I experience a sort of 're-experience'. I live with a deep awareness of what is likely to be. This is not from a database so it may be difficult for you to imagine. I am balanced with it and I have no need to change anything that is beginning to unfold in advance. It gives me an objective viewpoint if anyone can ever have such a thing. I can see the event occurring for its relevance to those around me. This is living in a love with deep reasoning, seeing why an event has a meaningful purpose. Not everyone does but those who practise this are able to welcome events. You might think it's like watching the past coming towards you, but it's a wonderful unfolding which embraces you. It's not intrusive when you feel it's not.

Living with likely outcomes is a different way of experiencing the moment. To you, it might feel as if the now is stretching its span. What I describe is not the same as seeing timelines; information about those will follow later.

I know Robert is keen that we write about Orlacka and the Arcturian perspective of love because that differs again. She has different ways of thinking that are not the same as the ones I have described. I said to Robert that Orlacka's input would not be helpful at this stage and her perspective will be more easily accepted in later submissions. It is good that he not only hears me well but knows me beyond the need to trust.

What comes to mind when I say the word alien? Perhaps extra-terrestrial types that use technology for their own divisive ends or benevolent races observing man's transition.

What was very unlikely to come to mind when I said the word alien was 'alien consciousness' and its interaction with your consciousness at lower and higher dimensions'. You are reading those interactions now, as they clearly exist between 'myself Antemedi' and 'myself Robert'. Awareness of consciousness can change and develop new fruits.

There comes a time of harvest if it is wished for. A seed that is sown grows into a plant, which produces more seed and, like the soul, it lives to express. Are the sweet fruits more cherished or they enhanced by their difference to sour? Yet some fruits can be so sweet they are sickly on the palette.

You might think that is an unusual analogy. It is one of several I shall give, but though it seems out of context it has connotations on several levels. Could you find one word to sum up what this analogy means? Perhaps you would need to invent a word for the blending of the sweet and sour of love and evolution that 'just is'. I am trying to unfold 'feeling an understanding' or new ideas. You do not have words for some of our concepts and feelings. If you do not know them then you cannot describe them.

Or can *you*?

In order for that possibility to exist it means *you* have access to your multidimensional self. At those levels, *you* will understand different concepts and have the relevant words. But what if I turned this all on its head and said that descriptions were a waste of time? Then everything I had said up until now would become pointless. That's probably an unexpected twist in the journey!

Let me show you that I am not deranged but alien. By now you see how your database and subconscious create and inform your choices. It would be fair to say that descriptions are part of the information they contain. We have been widening the description of 'yourself' to include multidimensional selves. It was not possible to describe them without unfolding the awareness that they exist. In which case we can say that a lack of knowledge informed the previous description of yourself.

Again, that is a description of your current perception. Since saying descriptions are a waste of time, I have used the word description continuously in all my sentences. *You* cannot function without description. It informs most of what you do. In the face of this, how can I continue to assert that 'description' is so restrictive it wastes time? Because that's the difference between our perceptions. This is why analogies and metaphors are so necessary. We could say that an analogy is another description and I am using it for a specific purpose to impart information. Yet, my position remains unaltered and so I suspect does yours. There are chasms between some of our ideas, so understanding each other isn't straightforward. I will, however, be showing pathways of understanding that can bridge the gaps, even if you remain routed on one side of the divide.

The difference we are presently encountering is 'primary focus'. You stand in a place and put your focus on to the particular thing you wish to focus upon. You don't need to remain in the same perspective all the time because there are many standpoints from which you can look at an object. You can then describe any differences from alternative viewing points. Having a wide variety of descriptions is like 'trying to know the object from as many views as possible', and in doing so you have captured its essence. The feeling of an understanding is not the same as understanding. What you feel is very important to what you understand, and distortion between the two creates unbalanced objectivity.

We can see this with Victorian naturalists who felt close to 'the understanding of their items' in their collections – merely by having them in the same room. They had captured not only the animals but their essence as well. Of course, studying the animals increased knowledge and there was a great desire to understand, describe and capture. A sense exists in your psyche about the power of knowledge and that to gain more is a good thing.

But I would contend in many instances you are just gaining more description. You have functioned well with this as your program, which you believe, has flexibility because you can change descriptions.

I still stand by what I said. There may be many descriptions in your database in the bag that continues to grow. You could say there are many descriptions upon which to stand and this gives many viewpoints to look at something. So, can you freely look at what you don't know?

If you let go of your descriptions, your focus would be fluid it would have nowhere to look from – it could be nowhere or everywhere at the same time. You could look at what you don't know and 'understand or know it' without the need to describe it.

Whatever you look at in the world is a reflection of yourself.

When you do not look to see yourself, as yourself – the world will have nothing of you or your thoughts to reflect back to you. When you are no-thing – nothing – you have no reflection in a mirror. You describe yourself and in your world you are something, so the universe reflects that back to you – a feedback of energy.

In order to release the tight hold you have on believing who and what you are, I shall pull apart some of your words. Everyone clearly wants to be 'something' and not nothing (extinct). But why a thing? An object an item of *description*. You are energy love and expression, you are not a thing. The Isness cannot be described in fullness and you are part of it the Isness. It is you and you are it, therefore you are also beyond description. Your energy and consciousness have such potential that neither you nor I would be able to conceive or comprehend it in fullness. It is never full nor is it empty, it is unlimited potential unless you experience it as restricted by whatever program or *way* of thinking you use.

I am trying to impart that these levels of perception are a more complete way of understanding and knowing while being in a certain state of mind as well. If you can see yourself as fluid beyond description – beyond the need to describe – you become more at one with that which you cannot describe. You can then know it by being at one with it.

In this way, access to universal information and other possibilities is not limited.

The universe is information and it is you, so all you need do is be the information. You, my friends, are not limited in your potential – you are only limited to what you believe is your potential. It is a very different place from where to live and operate. There are subtleties in what I have said that you may not have seen or understood. But I can assure you that the *way*

I think and live is very different on this side of the divide.

With this information, I hope you can begin to see why descriptions or the descriptive state of mind can be restrictive at this particular level of Andromedan thinking. Oh, and the fruit in the metaphor; replication of what appears to be the right way for the right purpose because that seems to be the nature of the world or the universe. The seed is the information, the *description,* for the fruit trees to follow in their growing programs. It seems fruitful to continue using the same ways even if some fruit is too sweet or too sour and not fit for purpose. If it is not badly broken, do not fix it. Your world is thus and so are you by the way you think.

The more you come to understand love, then the more you know it exceeds *description*. It's not a greater love – that would be putting a value on it – then it becomes description and restriction again.

### Different levels

Will I need to use description and information to talk about different levels? Yes, in part; that's because your present consciousness can't access the information by the knowing of information through its present type of connection to the Isness. I will use description to explain this information but the crucial point is this knowledge was not sought or found through description and data. I am mindful that to understand our level from yours requires the use of feeling sensors as well as intellect.

Your present awareness inhabits your plane with a veil of forgetfulness. It is one of your consciousness programs, and the 'apparent separation' stops you receiving conflicting information from other realms. Your world is a level of consciousness, and within it, there are levels of consciousness from murderers and drug dealers to the Dalai Lama. Suffice to say, the vibrational levels of people can be very wide. What each of you perceives of your world is a reflection of yourself and your description of who you are.

You know that 'like attracts like' and this happens on a vibrational level. You can feel and know the divisions of levels in your dimension, but they are only one small section of a much wider waveband. There are even lower vibrational levels with some pretty nasty entities, but unless you vibrate in a similar way or you want to go there you are going to be as safe as you currently are. You might think that fear of the unseen lower levels will keep you away from devious desires, but it is really a matter of vibrational equality. Those low levels feed upon themselves or on the energy generated by very low-level light beings. Connections can occur to humans if they have an excess of negative thought energy. Those negative thought energies coagulate (like to like) and can appear as a separate entity. But it is a collection of your counterpart subconscious programs.

Jung's term 'shadow self' is an ideal description of that. Usually, it is through this negative part of self that connections are made to the lower realms, so fear of it will not keep you any safer. These connections can be for karmic reasons, and if you know anyone who has such an attachment you will know how draining it is. Destructive energy will consume itself if left to its own devices. These are rare situations and you are protected by your aura, which is also a multidimensional energy field.

Going in the other direction, one of your expressions is, 'They light up the room when they enter,' this describes the faster-vibrating energy existing in that person.

The light on higher planes above you can create a pull, an

aspiration and a need to belong to something greater. Part of that is the feeling of going home, which is going back to yourself or higher levels of self. The pulse is active on those levels with higher intensity of information. Higher dimensions have form and purpose but the rules, programs and parameters, which they follow, are different. The soul experiences and the *ways* that entities think also reflect the programs; they are intertwined.

You and the universe have different vibrational levels. Your other dimensions don't sit there like empty voids waiting for you to evolve and activate them. They are alive and actively involved in their own way of being as well as interacting with you. How much knowledge of that you have in your present awareness is about what you can perceive and accept as being possible. In some cases, it would appear that knowing it would have no benefit.

For your consciousness to reach higher dimensions, complete with its awareness, requires a degree of tuning up. What you see or encounter is dependent upon your vibrational resonance, though it's also possible for entities to tune down and project to you. Humans can think or meditate themselves to higher levels, but they do not often fully engage with their consciousness existing on those levels.

Our perception of you in that state will be fuzzy incomplete energy. We can, however, engage with your 'higher dimensional self' and that part of your consciousness will undertake guidance for the whole of itself. This is one of the ways we are consciously engaging with many of you.

As you vibrate faster, your present awareness will change and vice versa. Time will feel different as if it need not exist – there is time enough for all things at a soul level.

The *me* you are listening to at this particular moment is still

Antemedi – but from one of my higher soul levels. When I say it that way, it makes it sound like I am not him in his dimension or that you are engaged with a part of his higher consciousness he is not fully aware of. Not so – it is all a matter of focus and what is relevant to the experience in the moment. He lives and experiences in his ways – in the ways that I have been talking about. I am him; I know all of him as I know all of Robert, for they are me. It may seem confusing to you but it's not – it's just knowledge that's on the edge of human comprehension. Who is who, after all, and at what level and when? These are the same questions and prompts I used earlier. By the time you read the last page of this book, you should be more able to understand those questions and the consciousness programs that interact and create.

You vibrate faster when you do not *describe* yourself, otherwise, you will keep to a narrow railway line rather than being fluid.

**R:** I am now struggling a little I don't know which bit of me is where and aware of what!

**A:** That's the point isn't it? It's all one and the same and you are superimposing or trying to describe or ascribe meaning to it – to fit it into the picture you have already. I am using my consciousness to talk to myself (you) in another level of consciousness experience.

The reasons for me to remain unknown to you are no longer necessary for your life purpose. It may not be easy, but you can know me as I know you because I am you. Furthermore, because you are looking at this in an unhelpful way it doesn't mean it has to be difficult. That is a perception – you are still trying to see new knowledge through old knowledge.

**R:** I have a lot of questions running through my mind but I know they will slow down reception.

**A:** Listen attentively even when new information seems strange. It is very difficult for you to see me as I see myself. For a start, you still inhabit your earth body despite being able to visit other levels in your mind and heart.

You are a little confused about me, Antemedi, in my 'functional form' and me in my functional form on a faster dimension level where I have switched focus to speak to you from. Your questions arise: 'Which higher consciousness program are you conversing with? Does the functional part of me have to be fully conscious of everything?'

To help let's look at that from your experience. You reprogram your subconscious and let it work for you – you create or change programs and let them run. The program is the programmer, it is a *way* of thinking. You are the program and the programmer.

Your questions came from a desire to define yourself and that created restriction. You were putting your energetic programs at arm's length, and you were not fully accepting that they are as much *you* as is love and soul. It's not easy to accept that you are a program.

All parts of Antemedi speak to you – he is multidimensional so many aspects will be involved. Yes, it would be much simpler to say you are speaking to him/me as an individual.

Because that's comfortable, it doesn't mean you should miss the opportunity to see more. Being fluid will allow you to consciously enter greater depths of multidimensionality beyond your current understanding.

# TWO

Arksar talks about the original universal energy that evolved from a paradox containing all and nothing. He calls it Mowhar and ascribes feelings to the now-defunct aspect that formed into the self-sustaining pulse energies of different dimensions.

**Robert (R):** That was an interesting way to achieve some of your aims, by showing how our own consciousness programs interact with each other. It reminds me of when people meet a deity such as Michael of the Blue Ray – or Archangel Michael (as he is commonly known) – they are having a personal interaction experience, but it's with that being's consciousness programs. That is why so many people can meet and interact with a deity.

**Antemedi (A):** Yes, true, but what you have said is from your earth perspective. In your language, 'program' removes person or spirituality and leaves a stale electronic computer term. "Etena Quanah", I would say as my expression for such an interaction, but again that has no reference for you. If our words have no meaning for you, what good is that?

At the moment I am introducing wider meanings and feelings to the words you use. That may be a little laborious but at least I can impart something deeper.

If I say that you are an 'entity', that seems to negate soul from the equation. Your word 'soul' has limiting descriptions attached to it so in order for you to grasp the next concept we will use the word entity.

**R:** At this point, Arksar, Orlacka and Aqueena appear around me as I am typing.

**Arksar (AR):** All things must change in order for there to be real change. Humanity has been held back, its time is here. You are not who you think you are and you no longer need to forget. By saying the word 'entity' Antemedi has widened the subject so we can talk about 'multidimensional entity'. We will bring our own individuality and outlook to help with this unfolding.

**R:** Entity is something that exists separately from other things and has a clear identity of its own, whereas soul by your definitions is interconnected to all and is multidimensional. Entity seems to be a divergence from what you have previously said about soul and unity of all.

**AR:** At the start of this presentation, you and Antemedi gave a good introduction to duality, also known as paradox. My words after this sentence may sound like a feeble explanation but the fullness will follow.

You are soul as well as entity. You are both and neither and all of them; it's just a matter of perspective. However, your perspective can change from the ones you currently hold. It doesn't mean the previous ones were wrong, merely that new information allows you to see them differently.

I am an entity, as are you, and when we meet we can interact from the perspective of being separate entities. If you choose to forget that you are united and connected, you create a self-experience.

When you try to feel the truth of union from a position in separation, you will not be able to. Only within union will you be able to experience the feeling of full union.

Union will clash with what you currently believe because you feel you are an entity.

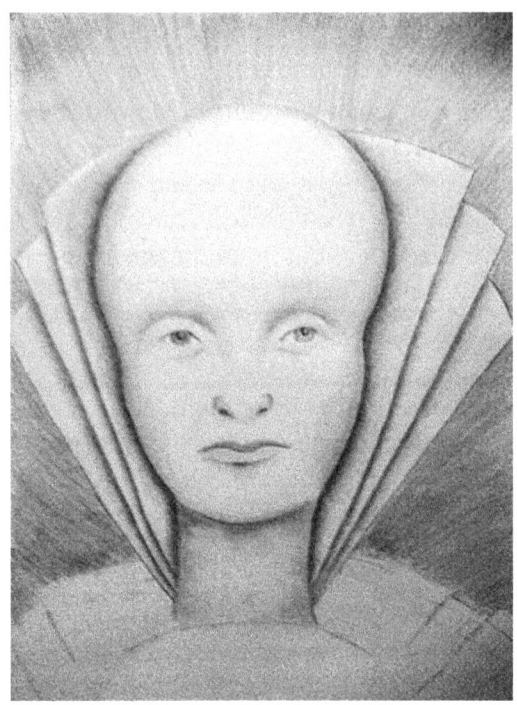

*Portrait of Arksar by Janette Oakman*

From separation, it feels like there is no point in union or even that it's possible. Great mystics have already unfolded some of this information about your nature, but it has little relevance or meaning to you or cultural life. The you includes all of you and the typist of these words. By forgetting union and embracing separation, it has given you a vast range of experiences.

Being told that 'you are all one' might feel as useful as an evaporated raindrop in a desert. The feeling of oneness all of the time is different from any sporadic feelings that you have of it from time to time.

I am not talking about the Andromedan communing or

even Orlacka's Arcturian trans-dimensional abilities. I want to show you how the universe is an entity not just a mass of energetic interactive programs.

I shall use emotional story-telling terminology. Do not disregard this simplicity because, by the end of the story, I hope you shall feel the magnificence of Mowhar and understand the concept of what she was.

Mowhar: Mother of all things: the one that unites; the one that is expansive; the one that gave birth and generated the pulse. We can trace the unlimited potential in all the dimensions back to Mowhar. She is not god, she had no interest in such things – she is the beginning of the beginning. She slept 'unaware' that she slept for more years than could be remembered. Until one moment she awoke and became the first creator – the creator of the pulse. To some in the old stories, it was as if she screamed.

The vibrations penetrated beyond the ideas of herself, beyond even the idea of boundaries. It was the birth and the death of her. She awoke and then fell back into nothingness. She was a paradox. She was and she wasn't.

**R:** Oh, that's so moving – I can feel the intensity of the awakening then the realisation that she could not exist and that she was born to die. Presumably, there are some parallels to pulse 'here and not here'?

**AR:** These are the old stories of my Cormaynian race passed down from when we do not know. It is also a residual memory vibration, still reverberating in every part of the pulse in the universe. That is why you felt it as you did. An awakening of awareness – a joyous expansion and the sorrow of death.

Several years ago, during May 2015, Antemedi had a conversation with you about pulse and you shared this in a website article *Colombeye all that is universe*. He told you that the start was like a spent casing, which formed the pulses of different dimensions. Over a longer period, this was explained as initial creator pulse and you were given diagrams to conceptualise shapes of pulses, which you have also shared. The pulses formed to have their own self-sustaining energies. Their repeating pulses did not need a starter or creator pulse anymore. If starter pulse or Mowhar continued its initial creation, then initial creation would last forever and all there would be is initial creation. The universe would be chaos with continuous initial creation.

The old stories say that Mowhar died so that her children could live forever. These stories show that she was an entity until she wasn't. We need to be careful with words used to explain the self-perpetuating dimensional pulses as 'on-off' and not use 'born-die'. But on the basis of what I have told you, that is not the case with Mowhar. While these are ancient stories about the initiation energy, they do help to partially understand the process.

The science behind this initial creative program or formula is exceptionally complex. In part, it's because a paradox is difficult to work with – it will reflect back to you any tool or thought you try to understand it with. You can't fully encapsulate the concept of 'never-ending potential' because you will never get there. How can you comprehend that 'trying to understand' has no such ability? A paradox cannot be understood with an enquiring mind. One understanding of it is that it has no understanding at all. Instead, you can just allow the paradox to 'be of importance' and 'no importance'.

The entity Mowhar is the universe, but Mowhar can no longer exist in the form as the creator of creators. It is not so much her children that live on, as it is herself. It was as if the entire total potential for joy was her but so was all the suffering. Mowhar was a paradox. Only from a paradox could

Mowhar come forth. That is what she was – she was the paradox – is and is not. Perhaps you can begin to feel this understanding – there would have been nothing without 'is and is not'.

This union of opposing ideals or forces is a theme that has been reflected in discussions about thoughts and feelings, levels of conscious, higher realms and, of course, you being all these things. Because the dimensions of the universe were created from paradox, they contain paradox in every part of *pulse, information, harmonics, matter, souls and soul enlightenment.*

Even feeling is Mowhar, but she no longer exists – not in the sense you can understand existence. She could not exist other than as a paradox without life and, paradoxically, she could only exist as a creative expression. That is not like your life or any kind of life that you could comprehend. We all have paradox within us, but not the initiation or creator paradox. Why re-create the creation that would be paradoxical like the birth and death of Mowhar?

We are all Mowhar reborn, we cannot go back to the union of paradox to any or all of that – it could not even be conceived. A baby cannot return to its mother's womb after it has taken its first breath. We rejoice in her death in joy and pain we love her because she is you and us. This is not the 'big bang' as your theorists put forward. The universe will not fall back in on itself, that is to assume it came from one particular point when in fact the centre of all is everywhere. The universes did not come from chaos but from ultimate paradox. Perhaps it might help if you envision this as 'energy and its own opposite energy'.

## Individuation

Antemedi touched upon individuation and the human experience of subdivision. One of your beliefs is that you would find the answers to the big questions about your existence and the universe by dividing things into the smallest common denominators – perhaps in that way you could find source. Though as you can now see, source is paradox.

Your meaning of individuality is part of your subconscious programs but it can be corrupted, leading to thoughts about 'the actual division of self and loss of self'. Paradox or duality also divides your subconscious (the seesaw beam). Scientific disciplines and the search for even more that is divisible throws up good discoveries. But the same does not apply to you as an individual. You do not create more of you when you divide yourself. Your sub-consciousness is the repository for much of the divided feelings and rationale.

Of course, you have the ability and the limitless capacity to do whatever you wish. Humanity experienced 'forgetting its full self' and in part, this was by agreement with negative forces. But in this blindness, man carried the 'separation program' on his shoulders as he marched forward at an unstoppable pace to find the 'all' in the 'smallest'.

That is why you (Robert), on one of your spiritual journeys, had the experience of ultimate self-division. To reach and know what was at the bottom of yourself. Wanting to know all and everything of yourself that you could.

**R:** That was a terrifying experience. In reaching for the understanding of all, I could not ignore the smallest. I wanted to know what was at ultimate division and I bloody well found it because you helped me!

**AR:** It was something you wanted to do and we also helped you return. The belief behind this was that if you could find the worst of you then you could extinguish it and no longer be fearful it might exist. The potential for something bad in you would never be known unless you searched for it.

So, we helped you cut away the overlaying thought programs in order that you could do that.

**R:** Your advice at the time was very insistent that there was no need to look, but I felt I could not rest until I had found out for myself. It began by sinking deeper and deeper into my lower consciousness.

By giving up my conscious or present self, I began to feel there was less and less of me. I felt smaller and smaller. I was either giving away parts of myself or they were being taken away. The plummeting increased exponentially and I became extremely frightened. I was being pulled apart and I thought, *I am going to become extinct, destroyed for all time.* When I got to what felt like the smallest part of me, the last piece, I wept and I pleaded: "I cannot be divided anymore, there is nothing more to give, what do you want from me?" It felt as if I was in the presence of some all-consuming negative entity. It seemed to last for eternity, time had been taken away and this was it – forever in some endless torture – the intensity of isolation was unbearable – there was nothing else and no one.

I was helped back (thank you), and when I looked at my watch only a few minutes had passed; so very different to my experience. I wasn't able to take on board your explanation until the following day when I had been calmed.

The only way I could find out if there was a hidden negative part of me was by removing all and everything of me that was good. In this way, it would reveal that which was not good. But the power of thought and creation also acts in duality. So instead of seeing myself pull me apart as if I was an observer, I became the experience instead. The being with whom I pleaded was me; it was my energetic thought to remove all that was good and have the experience.

My thoughts in paradox; I wanted to find what was left so all good was taken away – I created the experience. There was nothing evil or negative hiding and I could not be divided any further and yet my sponsoring thought was still saying, *Take all that is good away*. That was the feeling of becoming extinct.

**AR:** It would have been difficult for you to get there and back without our help, but we respected your needs and wishes.

**R:** I wouldn't recommend it as an experience and no way would I do it again. But it certainly stopped any thoughts that answers could be found in the ultimate division. I had reached the wrong end of the telescope. The point to all this? Perhaps there is none. There is no need to be inside a telescope to look from either end – the two vantage points are fixed viewpoints of a paradox. They will only show you the other end but, ironically, you don't ever see the other end because the inside lenses reflect back to you yourself. It will only show you where you are looking from. Pointless when you know – but I suppose the point is to know that – and that's a paradox.

**AR:** I think I led you into that nicely – from the creator pulse of Mowhar the paradox – to splitting current duality or paradox into its smallest part only to find that it is still YOU and you are still Mowhar paradox.

We do have calculus theories but technical information cannot connect you or make you feel any more connected to Mowhar. Formulas do not create feelings. If you can accept that Mowhar is gone and we are a reflection of her, then you have an understanding. We do use other paradoxical energies, and we have technical programs that work within the information fields to create them.

All of these we create within the existing dimensional pulses. This means we can use technology inter-dimensionally for all sorts of purposes. We thought it was useful to know that there are connections between technology and paradox in self-perpetuating flux.

As our theme is *'communication with the alien self'*, you now have an alien name for paradox. Perhaps instead of paradox you can use our word Mowhar to feel and express its greater depth as an entity, not a just a concept. After all, she is everywhere.

## Fresh information and new starts

**AR:** Let's begin at the start. We could say what particular start. Some starts are created by endings but is there such a thing as a fresh start? A change in direction is only the appearance of a fresh start. A makeover is not a fresh start. But is a start a beginning?

**R:** This is somewhat pedantic

**AR:** For good reason. You knew most of the subject matter transcribed from Antemedi in the early part of this book because you had worked on it before. We know the *way* your mind processes and accepts things that's why I am priming your consciousness.

You have kept to our advice to ask us questions and not to research material on the Internet unless you feel you have to. The Internet would take you in different directions to the ones we have planned. It also informs or distorts the way you interpret what we say because you will compare it to external data. It is beneficial to receive information as we present it because we know you and can see from a forward position.

This leads me back to the ground I was preparing for you – fresh information and a fresh start. It is not fresh information for your other layers of higher consciousness. We could say it's starting to have an effect but you will have no idea until I tell you what 'it' is. In this instance, it is you – in the singular sense and the wider human collective.

While there are more people awake, generally, your

societies' soul-level communications with other races do not appear in human waking consciousness. There is an overriding desire to meet us in the flesh as opposed to mental communication. You have lots of different races on earth so you should be able to comprehend that there are also many different types of alien humanoid. My race, Cormay, is very small in numbers and acts under the umbrella of the Andromedans. The best form of introduction is usually a gentle process. Andromedans have made themselves known in the flesh to some contactees and helped retrieve alien life memories for others. There will be more open contact but it will be when and with humans of our choosing. That is not to say we are manipulating but we do not wish to engage directly with certain political élites. Contact will be much greater after your transition.

Humanity will have its fresh start – the shift or the upliftment, as it's called, will change the basis of everything. Having outlined to *you* the dimensional and spiritual vibrations, *you* all will be more able to understand this fresh start. It will change your essence and affect your way of thinking. It is a fresh start not a rehash from your existing ideas. Depending on when people read this information, many things may have begun to unfold or have happened. Some people are aware of uplift's imminent arrival and have provided their own take on when and what is to happen. It was a shock to Robert when we said it would be instantaneous.

Of course, there is a build-up till a critical mass is reached but the critical mass required is actually quite low. Not only does the earth have consciousness but so do the other planets and your sun – it is the same for the rest of the universe. Plans or consensus will form by many layers of consciousness interacting with programs. Time is a 'when' and when is defined by windows of events as they change. These events will happen and the harmonics of the earth will change. The information will change in the on-off pulse so it will be instantaneous. This means physical matter will alter slightly and so will DNA and your consciousness. It is all part of a greater universal agreement. Perceptions will change as veils fall and blockages disperse. Senses shall be heightened and you will just know more than you did before. It will be easier to know if someone is being untruthful and it will be easier to challenge that which is unacceptable. There will be no hiding, for corruption will be seen as it is.

We will be able to help with several technologies and free energy generation if that is your wish. You have that ability already but it is withheld for financial and control agendas. These uplifts will challenge financial structures and those that have the most to lose.

The upgrade or higher frequencies shall affect your subconscious programs, which will be partially re-set. You won't think in quite the way you used to. Your thoughts will be more community based than selfish. You will still be you, but it shall be as if the sun shines on a new spring morning with many old and false concerns gone. A few may struggle and wish to remain as they were, but they will have choices to mentally locate elsewhere. Some may wish to leave their earthly bodies and a few will 'disappear' by their own free will. At the moment, karma is seen as the consequence of what you do in one lifetime, you face in another. It is an often misunderstood form of cause and effect. It is more about the energy you create by your deeds – that energy belongs to you because you created it. It's what you then do with the energy that matters. A murderer doesn't have to become an innocent victim in another life.

Cause and effect will be faster with little delay.

Duality still affects your spiritual growth within your current mental constructs and programs. An example would be: 'You can never understand betrayal unless you have been both the betrayer and the betrayed.' Often these patterns repeat even if the understanding is there; then they become more cause and effect. There is no karmic debt, just your energy, which you are responsible for. In the case of the example above, when you take charge of the energy with love, the need to be on either side of betrayal falls away from your life experiences. It no longer has relevance and it just isn't there for you.

One of your difficulties is being locked into a collective consciousness program that tells you to repeat deeds and actions when you no longer need to. Karma then becomes run-repeat consciousness, which has been manipulated by negative forces.

The subconscious upgrades in the uplift will mean that you do not need to repeat patterns and you can step outside some of them. Your negative vibrations will reduce and you will have a finer light body of energy. Your mental agility and psychic abilities will increase, allowing greater communication with other beings.

Like Antemedi I shall keep my focus on communication and not delve further into the subject of the shift. However, it was necessary to show its great impact on your ability and *ways* of communicating not only with aliens but also humans.

## Direct communication

**AR:** What do we mean when we think about direct communication? We on this side and you on the other? Telephones, real-time video or meeting face to face is a very narrow bandwidth. It excludes intuition, the deeper 'knowing' sixth sense to the five (sight, sound, touch, taste and smell). This sixth sense can contain all of the preceding five and include information and ideas as well. You are all likely to have had such experiences. You might remember when you smelled a cigar or a rose, only to find there were no smokers or flowers nearby. You might have seen something out of the corner of your eye or heard strange voices. These five senses in the sixth can be quickly dismissed in order that 'normal life can continue'.

Have you ever thought of someone only to find they telephone you in the next moment? How often has your space been invaded – you feel it because someone has moved into your closer auric energy. You might say personal space is more to do with what you find consciously acceptable. However, if someone were to approach you stealthily from behind you would still know they were there.

The point I am bringing you to is about the value you place upon the different types of communication and how that affects your use of them. Lack of familiarity doesn't help and some imply that 'knowing' is not to be trusted. They say it is the home of charlatans disguised as clairvoyants. To be fair, some are, but there are discord and duplicity in many other areas of life as well.

There is a sense you might not be able to trust this self-inner knowing. You may doubt that you have it or that you won't be able to use it. When you observe from a place of doubt, you will superimpose it upon what you see. It's the same as putting the word fear on a pair of spectacles; whatever you see in the world you will see through that.

Now, 'doubt' is very interesting because you believe that it has a use. It is valid to ask, "Have I got this right? I need to check it through." Checking is a form of reassurance and that is something warm and comforting to seek. Doubt and reassurance are bedfellows in duality. Doubting your decision is 'doubting yourself', which is then projected onto the outside world.

Because psychic attributes are not often used, they have become flabby. Like all things, there are a few pitfalls. Wishful thinking can influence what you think you want to see. The example of Robert's thinking and wish to remove all good to see what might be hidden is a prime example. It also shows the power of the mind, but the experiences it brings are not necessarily revealed in the way you had hoped. They do, however, reflect the initial sponsoring thoughts or desires.

What I have said might undermine thoughts of expanding these abilities. But such thoughts and feeling are preconditions or 'preference settings', which affect the outcome. A clear mind and heart are ideal but not always necessary. The objective way to proceed would be to keep things simple, trusting that what comes is meant for you. The universe is you and it loves you, it will give you what you need. Of course, what you need is totally different from what you may want upon your platform of desires.

My definition of direct communication would be 'direct communication with yourself'. In this way, you are connected to everything else and not dependent on a third party. There is nothing to fear from getting in touch with yourself. You may encounter your own interpretations of 'fear programs', but if you remember to see them as programs, they have less of an effect on you.

Direct communication can be used for many things: self-healing; accessing information; problem-solving; positive/creative thinking; freethinking; relaxation; distant viewing; human psychic interactions, and inter-dimensional contact.

Your mind and heart are very powerful tools, and they can

be used in positive ways. So, I am giving a short list of methods that can be used at your level to assist or experience life differently.

Observing the mind is quite a simple process; in a similar way to meditation, you disengage the gears that connect you to the subconscious program. There are lots of books or YouTube videos that give guidance on different techniques. In reality, you only need to be able to still the mind. Try not to search for anything or ask closed questions – just see what transpires. Don't worry if nothing happens; it's as much about knowing what is possible and gaining familiarity through practice.

**Inter-dimensional contact:** If you would like to link with us but feel the need for a little assistance, then try the following YouTube videos: [5]*Antemedi Andromedan perspective 6* and [6]*Antemedi Andromedan perspective 7*. (See References for links to these videos.)

These are guided meditations and are pathways of light that can be followed. The more people that travel on them, the more energy is added. These mental pathways link to the consciousness on our levels. What you see or interpret will be specific to you, and you can do this as many times as you like.

Another way is to set an intention such as *I would like my guides to help me see a safe alternative realm of benevolent beings.* After stilling yourself, imagine you are coming out of your physical body and floating above it. See yourself moving upwards, out of your house, looking at the roof, then at the landscape as you move higher. Drift up through the clouds until the earth gets smaller; keep floating away until you feel you can't go any further. Know in your heart you are somewhere safe, and look around you – take it gently and see what forms in your mind. It's possible to be in another realm with other light beings or on a craft or biosphere. If you do this with your spirit guides,

77

then the people you meet are likely to be connected to you in some way.

**Self-healing:** You can mentally locate yourself inside an organ or a part of your body that is causing you discomfort. It is similar to the previous floating away, but this time you move your focus inside yourself. Much illness relates to problems of energy, and disease is mind and body not at ease. Diseased thoughts are primarily energy and information, so they affect the information fields that instruct the formation of your body matter. With practice, you will find that your body speaks to you from its level of consciousness. Often it will be metaphorical images and stories, designed to be understood in the way it knows best. It is also a good way of healing the subconscious 'seesaw' energies and thought processes.

**Accessing information:** Your first thought might be that the Akashic records hold all the information you need. But don't forget that self-healing is accessing information about yourself. The hall of Akashic records is a place to focus upon – a construct or program that can be used for a specific purpose. I will expand on this shortly. The ability to access information boils down to intent and sponsoring thoughts, which are not always seen. Is your purpose honourable with loving intent? If it isn't pure, you will get back a reflection of your desire or a meaningless jumble. Your higher self is aware of desires and it is unlikely to allow a connection to information that could be exploited.

**Problem-solving:** You have seen the importance of intent when expanding your communication because it influences outcomes. Problem-solving depends on the type of problem; for example, if it's inter-personal then see *Human psychic interactions* (one of the follow on headings).

Let us say your cat has gone missing and, depending on

your skill level of stillness, you might be able to sense where it is. However, if you needed to have an emotional experience of cat loss it's unlikely to work. If you are a natural worrier, you are unlikely to find kitty through such a program, as it will influence what you sense. Why not explore the reason behind the excessive worry? All that you are will filter what you see.

Stilling the mind can help solve problems, but it will not necessarily give a direct solution if you need to have the experience of the problem.

If you have a desire to overcome problems, you will see events as problems in order to overcome them. The more you see problems the more you have the opportunity to overcome them. Consequently, you may solve many problems, which on the face of it seems to be a good thing. These problems you will find located on your seesaw.

**R:** I remember a Mandarin sage came in several years ago to give his take on that. He said: "To every problem, there is a solution. The solution may be palatable or unpalatable. Then you may say that life is a series of solutions.

"The trouble with this is that solutions can only exist by virtue of a relationship to problems. Do not see life as problems nor solutions but as a series of experiences from which to learn. Accept them with love because they are given with and created by it."

While that is true, it's one hell of a statement to accept if your nearest and dearest have been mowed down in a road traffic incident.

**AR:** The problem with problems! You are now talking about sorrow and loss as being a problem. Many seek a reason why, but often the lack of an answer to that question becomes a problem. Many problems are more about the way they are seen and interpreted. I do not experience problems and they are not challenges to be overcome; that would create problems. I see outcomes from a position of love and acceptance and have no reason to avoid or to run from communally formed events. But, we digress.

**Positive or creative thinking:** This is where you imagine yourself having already found a parking space in a crowded street – also known as *cosmic ordering*. If it works in conjunction and in harmony with the universe, then so be it. You arrive as someone just leaves their space; it's all part of a consciousness program. It's also possible to view the area within your mind; the mind will then show you where spaces are.

But if the positive thinking comes from a desire to avoid the feelings associated with not finding a space, then it is more likely to be wishful thinking, and what you try to avoid will present itself.

If you play the lottery at some level, you wish to win. That's not winning. What you may not see is that you have created the experience of wishing to win. Winning or losing is secondary to the 'experience of wishing' that you have created.

But 'I will believe I have won,' isn't going to work either; that's pretence based in self-interest. Do you really believe it, or is it a mantra to repeat to help you win because there is doubt?

Imagining yourself as having won is the way, but it's still unlikely to work. Everybody else is also part of the same universe and it has to take their wishes into account as well. It is also easy to lose sight of the sponsoring thought and personal feelings behind the desire to win, as these also affect outcomes.

Positive thinking based in love creates more love for you; it also helps family, friends or the wider world. Light-workers do this differently – they can project or manifest energy to specifically help or heal a situation. It doesn't mean their energy overrides the recipient, but it can boost energies as well as helping thought processes.

**Freethinking:** This happens when you do not have a specific wish or outcome in mind. Ask yourself an open question which does not tie you to duality. "Please can you show me what I can do to help this situation." It removes the context that it's a problem and the desire for the outcome doesn't need to fit your database parameters. Your thinking is then free from personal desires. Not any easy thing to do if you are trying to solve a problem. Thinking free from your desires allows you to see different outcomes and different ways of achieving them. Obviously, you have to be in the right state of mind.

Objects can be observed in the mind by freethinking. You can rotate, look inside or see inaccessible areas. You can use it for interpretation or seeing what would otherwise be hidden. It can be useful with discoveries or inventions.

The Akashic records are said to contain all past thoughts and all future thoughts. That is another definition of the Isness. To have this as a library means you can walk into the building and look for a specific book on a particular theme to help you. This library is a mental construct filled with energy information – it is a tool but foremost it is an energetic program. It is a way to see something so that your mind can have access to it. It does and doesn't exist for us – we don't need to see information in that way in order to access it. For us, it is *intuitive knowing* or the flow and acceptance of information. Fluidity is where we know we are the information and in that way, it manifests inside us. That is our way of freethinking.

None of this information is about power, wealth or advantage; that is of no consequence. There are some earth humans who can reach these levels and have to be very

81

honest with themselves about the reasons they seek such information. These programs of information often have sub-programs, limiting access to only those seekers who have a clear intent.

**Relaxation:** You need to be relaxed to experience relaxation. It has an element of freethinking, but it's more about being at one with the oneness of yourself and the universe. You could bathe or swim in its energy. In your mind, you could walk from a sunny beach and feel the coolness of the sea.

You could go underwater without the need to hold your breath or sit in a lush garden overflowing with birds and butterflies. Try floating from one mountaintop to another. Whatever comes to mind, if this is what relaxes you. An alternative is to remain still and seek nothing – just be with yourself in moments of connection and peacefulness.

These moments of stillness can be used as energy restoration or regulation. For such an occasion you could lie down and ask for assistance. If this happens, you may feel tingling or muscles twitching. In this way, it can be a form of healing. Energy regulation is instantaneous for us because of our connections to finer levels of light energy.

**Distant viewing:** I only mention it in order not to exclude it as a psychic attribute. It is the ability to move the mind's point of awareness to a particular point of focus. Your governments have used it for espionage. Purpose, however, defines the outcomes, so your intent is what you create.

Loving intent means you can see with an *open focus*. It allows you to look at another person who might be on the other side of the world. Viewing their energy is best by permission and can enable access to information for healing or enlightenment.

**Human psychic interactions:** Light-workers who heal trauma in others practise open observational viewing, which can be used to heal as well as help seekers to evolve and move along their pathways. This form of sensing will become much easier after the uplift.

So, I would like to round off with ways to communicate that can be used practically for energy release and growth. It is something anyone can do providing it's used with love.

Let's say you have a problem with a family member and you are at an impasse, unable to see each other's point of view. You are both feeling wounded, so it is difficult not to act or create from those feelings. Bring to mind that you can meet with the energy of the other person but at a higher level of consciousness – one that is more considerate. With your eyes closed and in your stillness bring them into your mind and imagine they are in front of you. They can do no harm to you at that level of consciousness. Explain in gentleness how you feel and what makes you feel the way you do. This has several effects – you will know you are being heard – it will be easier to articulate and express yourself – you can let go of your fears and vulnerability and you will receive no physical reaction.

Having expressed yourself – wait for a response. You may find there is an acceptance of part of your views or suffering. In return, you will need to hear their feelings. If you are unable to interpret, allow yourself to sense or feel it. Know in your heart that they act from wounds or distorted subconscious. Remind yourself that it's a program they experience, and they are acting from that. If you can do so, accept and give understanding in love – see them as the person behind or afflicted by an energetic program. Offer them love to help with their program and you may in return receive love from them.

This really works on the energetic levels, and you will see this reflected in any subsequent physical meeting.

It's a good way of dealing with an aggressive person. It can heal deep wounds where you have been hurt on a regular basis. If you are afraid of such an individual, you could interact through an intermediary. In which case, bring someone else into your mind that would stand between the two of you. If the energy of your hurt was truly created by the other person, it actually belongs to them. Imagine a suitcase containing your hurt and pass it back to them or via the intermediary. This is cause and effect and it is only right that you do not keep holding for them that which is theirs.

# THREE

Antemedi uses metaphorical constructs to help us access and understand unknown information. He introduces timelines, explaining how we can experience them. (These themes are expanded in subsequent chapters). He shows what observer information feels like when partially removed from human constraints. Aqueena adds perspectives to enhance understanding.

**Antemedi (A):** Arksar skimmed through the last subjects quite quickly. I know Robert has concerns that it's not relevant to the theme *consciousness, communication and the alien self.* However, we believe it is important to share knowledge, not only about the way that you think but also the way that you *can* think. The human psyche can be alien to itself if it is only partially known. We are not meddling in your thought processing but sharing our knowledge of what is possible. I didn't say I would restrict it to comparisons between your current ways and ours.

**Robert (R):** I was concerned that some people might flounder if they tried a few of those techniques.

**A:** Indeed they will, but some of them will not. We can see your society evolving and becoming more at one with itself. Functioning with, as many internal communication processes as possible will allow a greater flow of external communication.

Arksar talked of Mowhar, the founding paradox energy.

There are many other types of energy. There is one that we call Siscilla. To explain that will require me to talk about timelines and all-time – or the moment of now.

We have already toyed with the ideas of starts and beginnings or if indeed, there is anything new. If all things are possible and nothing is new, it would mean they have already been thought of. Of course, that is paradoxical because we have always said the Isness is unlimited in potential, and that it is impossible to describe it in its fullness. Therefore, how can everything have been thought of? While the Isness is unlimited within you, you limit it and live within those boundaries. A little bit like putting reins on a horse.

**R:** Really?

**A:** Let me continue. By limiting potential you can see the direction in which you are heading. It gives contextual relationship when otherwise there would be everything and nothing, which seems confusing. I shall expand upon my metaphor about the horse; still your mind and let it appear.

Look at this wonderful beast, as it stands before you ready to ride. Put your feet in the stirrups and climb onto the saddle. There are no reins, just a saddle horn. She will take you on a journey into the universe.

**R:** We are on a flat plane composed of energy and energy lines; there is nothing but energy. The horse picks up speed and we hurtle forward, faster and faster, greater than any speed a horse could gallop. There are no jerky movements, just speed; the horizon remains in the same place and the plane never ends.

The horse is an energetic program and not bound by the physical. It will keep speeding forwards forever until it does not. So I bring it to a halt to have a look at the environment – we might as well while we are here.

Antemedi is standing where I have stopped. We are now so far away from where we began that we can't see the starting point. There is a strange feeling that we are where we always were despite the movement forwards. Looking backwards, we can see the energy of where we have been. Along our route are small packages and I wonder if they fell from the panniers on the back of the horse.

Out of inquisitiveness, we walk back over our route to collect them. Fairly soon, both our arms are full and more remain, so it's obvious we are picking up in excess of what could have fallen from the bags. Upon returning to the horse, we inspect the bags to find that the buckles are secure and nothing is missing. Something has been created as we moved through the Isness.

They look like cubes of golden energy but they are programs of information. They are placed at the intersections of long golden threads, which show the route we took with the horse. But as I scan around there are more travel lines than the original one we travelled on.

**A:** Let's take one of these energy programs and walk forwards, past where the horse has stopped. If you look ahead, you can see there are more energy programs on the ground in front of us. It's as if they have already been placed here; you can see other golden threads in all sorts of directions connecting them. If we look above us, we can see there is another flat plane similar to ours. It is clear like glass and we can see ourselves up there and we are doing the same things.

Looking below us, there is another plane where we can see the top of our heads as we replicate our movements. We are seeing activation on three levels with the past behind us and the future laid out in front of us. The fast, forward-moving horse created the appearance of the flow of time. Because it's no longer moving, we can walk backwards or forwards on our route, but it will still feel the same wherever we tread.

We can move quite a distance sideways to our right or left, but no matter how far we go, the horse is always within arm's reach when we look back for it. The experience is that of no distance – that distance does not exist. Everything you are or connected to is always with you and you cannot escape it or it from you.

Let us walk forward in front of the horse again. As we encounter the first energetic program, it will show an energetic presentation of us several feet in front. It's like we have come up behind ourselves where we would be in the future. If you look beyond this first program, you will see that there are more programs that stretch out in front of us. Each one has a series of mirrored images of us stretching out into the distance. As we walk on, we enter the next energetic program of ourselves and it feels just like us. As we proceed further, we meet ourselves again and again. They become us and we become them. We can now perceive that each version of us knows something different.

We will slow down our walking speed so our awareness can change. While we head in the same straight direction. every so often there will be a shimmer. It's an energetic doorway in which we automatically move sideways. What appeared to be a straight timeline travelled by the horse isn't so. The straight route is shifting, it has always been shifting. It has been imperceptible and you cannot see it unless you either know it is there or you have been shown it.

**R:** If we are going slower, are we covering distance at slow speed? Speed x distance = time taken, but I thought time had stopped here?

**A:** Movement does not have to relate to time, nor does movement have to relate to distance. This metaphor has been created for entirely different reasons. I have already shown that movement is an illusion in your realm. For this metaphor, we can use our word, *Silenka*. You do not comprehend what our word means, that's why I am showing you this long metaphorical explanation. Your questions are slowing us down.

**R:** Now that's funny because I am typing this on earth in flowing time, and I'm slowing you down where there is no time!

**A:** Indeed, but you are in the *perception of time*, which is a program, and anyway the grip of time is changing in your dimension.

In my metaphor, we are appearing to move because we have energy constructs around us that keep changing. In this construct, there are different versions of you and me. They may appear as energetic shadows to you, but in essence, they are the same as you.

**R:** But they are not moving.

**A:** Not for this particular exercise. If you look to our right, you will see we also have a mirrored reflection. If you wave you can see yourself waving also. All our movements are reflected back at us. But we can only see this happen because we are aware that we can.

Let us shift our focus to the original concept of open space and the energetic lines we started with. We are in the place we stopped and we are able to see more than 'one view' in the same space. It is the former and it is not both at the same time. What we see is what we choose to see. It is and it isn't – these are the same concepts we used in paradox but you are now able to see them as dimensions of different focus in the same place. As concepts and dimensions, they all exist in the same place.

I have changed what we see again, this is a new view. There

are reflections quite close on our left and right. It now feels like we are in a rectangular glass tunnel. But because we know these are holographic energetic reflections, our minds are not restricted by what we see – so we may pass through them.

As we walk through the side of this energetic tunnel, the reflections disappear. We have returned to the scene where we are in front of the horse, looking forward at the images of us in the future. However, we can now see that these different programs of our selves are also placed around us, not just in front. The images of both you and I are waiting for us to experience them. On closer inspection, you can see they are interconnected by the *shimmering energy*. It's the same energy as the fluid mirror glass or holograms, but more of a wisp or a shimmer because it slips us from one timeline to another – one version of us to the next as we experience life. There are no boundaries, but now we have the appearance of movement when we shimmer into another version of ourselves.

When we look at the realms above and below, they seem to have similar attributes – but they do not have the same focus or way of interpreting their environment program. They are within their own constructs but they are still us. The one below is unaware of us but the one above is looking down upon us.

Perhaps the one looking down on us is also a reflection of you and I, here and now?

**R:** It's your metaphor, you should know!

**A:** It is and it isn't and it can be both but this is your metaphor as well because you are me. Let's delve deeper into this explanation. All of these things are happening in the same moment. That may sound impossible and you may wonder how can your consciousness be split into so many parts.

**R:** I suppose that depends on how big or complex it is

90

**A:** Or how small! Big isn't necessarily the way to go; it's about how many selves or autonomous programs you can have. And, like the universe, that's unlimited; all you have to do is create them.

**R:** Wow, that really does show what unlimited potential is! Are we having the same moment over and over again but in a different form each time?

**A:** Not really. I am showing the evolution of a program. A program that changes its parameters – a program that thinks and has degrees of sentience. This is all you, it is the way you live and the way you are. The nuggets of energy are program alterations, changing your timelines and options around you.

**R:** But these are all reflections or possibilities of this me because I look the same.

**A:** If you had been bald in one, would you not be bald in another? Try to see everything around you as programs and energy – don't even see yourself – let yourself go – you are a construct.

**R:** Interesting – there is no need to understand the *just is* or *Isness*. In essence, we are all-peaceful and all-knowing. Yet I feel I do not know enough and I need to know more even though I am also *just is*.

**A:** Good, a desire to evolve and learn. That is one of the key parts of the program otherwise there would be little expansion of consciousness. While consciousness has expanded its possibilities, some parts of it have not.

**R:** Doesn't all of the soul eventually have to be evolved?

**A:** Not if it doesn't want to. But would you leave a part of your consciousness adrift in your subconscious, either causing chaos or creating negative energies? It would be like eating rotten food every day when fresh food is available.

I can see you are having problems with the concept of who is in charge of all this. The answer is no one and everyone. It is your particular way of seeing this new information. You are not interpreting it wrongly, it's just that it has many ways to be seen and experienced.

As well as self-experience, there is also the experience of observation. You can observe yourself from within the construct of you and from afar. From the self and from what appears to be another self.

If we float up and shift our focus to the dimension above, we are in a position to be aware of everything we were doing below. Take a moment to travel there with me. From this higher vantage point, we can look further ahead and see all the timelines laid out below. We could see the likely routes, which are more energised, or the variation possibilities. These routes will all end at the death of Robert on earth. Everything you do below on that plane you can experience here – but differently. Pick up one of the nugget programs and observe it. This higher plane is 'observer perspective'.

**R:** There is a feeling of being casually aware of the programs and feelings, but I am removed and somewhat distant. I am observing while away from that part of me that's active and living down there. This experience of observing is different from observing myself when I am actually in the experience. The struggles and programs on the level below do not affect me here. Love exists here, but it does not have to suffer and struggle with the same programs below. What is this casual feeling?

**A:** It is attached and not attached, it is the sense of observation that is not restricted by the programs below. When below, you believe you observe yourself. You see what you do and think and within that level of you, it feels like observation. It is a restricted observation, whereas here you feel detached from your reality. You feel like a casual observer, unaffected by the intensity of feelings because duality does not have its own hand and its own way. It exists, but we do not need to see things divided up. We see the wholeness of those paradoxes and they become something different again, which is quite gentle.

Look at yourself below, picking up another energetic nugget and, as observer here, do the same below. When you observe here, it has no hold over you – so you are neither drawn to it nor pushed away.

**R:** Bizarre. I wonder if it's similar to the feelings a baby has when it begins to experience the world around it.

**A:** Well, as an observer here of early baby life, it would have a few comparisons, but the 'here observer' will also change as they invest more consciousness during the growth of the child. There is an energy attached to each incarnate body called body life force, which keeps the body functioning and growing. That is an energy life force and a program of life force.

Gradually, more conscious awareness comes to the child and its consciousness begins to interact with your collective programs and, in that way, becomes more like you. Similar things happen during prolonged deaths. A dying person's body may appear to be in pain, but they are not always consciously aware of that pain. They are in an elevated consciousness program while the body life force is a program that just supports the body to keep it alive.

Consciousness used for observation here is not restricted nor is it dulled. I know you are referring to the feeling, the *free curiosity,* that exists at this level.

*(At this point, Antemedi's energy partially fades and Aqueena comes forward to greet me.)*

**Aqueena (AQ):** You are making more of this than need be. I can say that because you are. You think you will have difficulty understanding such unusual concepts, so you create that experience. You do not need to experience these presentations through that particular program. If we said to use the program 'easy'– that would cause different difficulties. There would be comparisons and 'more easy' would lead to wondering if what we explain is 'too easy' and those last two words diminish the value of the word easy and, of course, everything we say to you. Then, what we say may be simple and not worthwhile. Measurements and descriptions distorting the free flow of information.

An observer is not hampered by such subdivisions. It is neither easy nor hard – It doesn't have to be either.

With each word we say, you can understand more and more the nuances between the earth and the dimensions above. One of the purposes of these submissions is to show how and why thought programs hamper communication. The main issue will be humanity's interpretation of us and not the other way round.

So back to observation without constraints.

We created an image that looked exactly like you in order that you could feel comfortable being observer energy at this level of self. The 'earth dwelling and feeling' part of you was on a plane below in a different program. As you know, I am a part of your higher consciousness, and I previously explained that I also live my life as 'I wish to express'. I am not some entity whose sole purpose is to observe and guide you towards me. I wish to explain this more openly, but I would like you to enter a less tangled perspective before I do that. I am sorry that this communication is causing pain in your head, but we are pushing energy through some of your interpretation programs and database.

94

At the moment, to you, this realm seems detached and unconnected. In some ways that is correct because we are not directly connected to and immersed by your earth programs of interpretation. We are not like you and so you do not always feel connected to us, even though we are part of the same consciousness. I can assure you we are and that, as you progress, you will feel more attached and at one with our vibration. This observer sensation and interpretation will also change.

I have shown you some of the places where I work or relax. Neither of those words adequately describes my experiences and what I do. Work is a joy and, as a relaxation, it is also the other way round. On one visit I brought you to a council chamber/meeting room though those two words fall short of the full description. Some readers might think a council has more importance than a meeting, but that is an earth definition based upon a council having more influence or power. In that meeting, I appeared as a speaker giving a lecture to several beings including some earth shadow states of consciousness. Instead of *lecture*, let me use the word *interface* even though it has both computer and technology connotations for you. It is the unhindered exchange of concepts and feelings, without value, given to speakers or recipients. Everyone is equal in love, and the living consciousness programs allow interaction between any one of us or indeed for all.

On that occasion, we spoke about the energetic damage caused to the consciousness of animals during human warfare. A particularly destructive example was in the fields of Flanders where horses were emotional traumatised when their flesh was ripped and torn by ammunition. We explained that because humans created that energy, they had responsibility for it. What you create in energetic terms doesn't just go away by itself. Your world may be different from that now in the physical, but the trouble is when you only look at that one, you do not see the energetic worlds. As Arksar said about karma. "All that is energetically created exists until it is changed."

This example is only one of an unseen multitude of energies that affect your world. Your world energy may not seem dark to you, but to certain types of beings, it would be insufferable. To those with knowledge and wisdom of it, that's another matter.

The meeting showed the breadth of our awareness and the energies we choose to become involved with. This is not work in the sense that you define work – it is another way in which I choose to express myself.

We view such things with compassion, understanding and emotion but without emotional 'exaggeration' in the ways you do. With this explanation I am trying to harmonise your initial experience of observation, to settle it by showing you how it's used by me.

Observer Robert in this vibration has a different program to 'the earth you'. So when you are here, you can observe yourself in what seems a more 'dispassionate' or objective way. This consciousness observation program of yours sees things in energetic terms. Feelings, concepts, thoughts, or whatever you wish, can be seen without utilising duality, measurement and value.

We have taken you here before. We challenged you before by saying, "You are nothing – literally no-thing not even yourself." That is not a comfortable concept for anyone when presented with it for the first time.

After much arguing with Antemedi, you were more accepting, so he prepared a package of emotional information for you. You downloaded this and wrote without stopping for most of one day. In that day, you were more him than you. He put the constructs of being nothing and approaching nothingness into a format that you could easily accept. You are not who you think you are – you have no value and you are valueless.

**R:** Yes – thank you all for that. Perhaps a reader might be rather concerned at your last statement. To have no value and be valueless is quite soothing to me. It is having no need for value for measurement – for comparison. It is a freedom from value with no attempt to describe oneself. It made such a big difference, allowing me to be closer to you all through that process of accepting nothingness.

I am finding it difficult to explain the wonderful feeling I have of being of no value. It's as if you fully need to accept you have no value in order that you can let go of any value of yourself.

Only then can you live without requiring value. Your words and expressions may sound quite unusual to some readers, but they are heartening to me. Though, because of the earth consciousness, I don't often live in that state of mind.

**AQ:** Those particular words from Antemedi were designed for you after being aside from us for so many years. It was not an abrupt introduction, but nonetheless, it did not sit so easily at first. However, we are pleased that you shared the experience of the download from him in [7]The Boy, the Beast and the Nothingness (See References for YouTube link). It was a watershed in your consciousness while it was still constrained by earth programs. It also detached you from the construct of belonging to anything, including yourself; it enabled you to hear us from where we currently are.

It has already been said that higher levels of self have lives of their own as well as having the life of you. Try to let go of the idea that my consciousness is split into separate entities, and instead see that I undertake different tasks at different points of focus. This includes being able to talk to myself at many levels – this is the way we all are.

I can see you pondering about your evolution, wondering if on death your energy increases and you join or become these higher aspects like me? After all, we have said you are an idea of who you are and the representative energy of that. How many more times would you like to reincarnate – when, where and as what? Some future upgraded earth, perhaps; past or future lives as another type of humanoid?

There are timelines in timelines and overlays to overlays, but as I give this explanation it makes you feel even more detached; that you are some pawn or whimsical subterranean expression of a mass consciousness. You understand most of the things we present to you. We give you more, but that doesn't mean every time we do so you shall feel lost. This ties in with the way you need to see these conversations and disclosures as being difficult. Instead, it can be about knowing. There will always be something more to know until you do not wish to know any more.

**R:** You are speaking in riddles.

**AQ:** You can see it that way if you wish, but it's information that you presently cannot contextualise within your mind. It's not difficult, it's not necessary to feel lost or insignificant, they are not of the essence of what I am saying.

**R:** You know my thoughts, for which I am glad, and your presence warms me when the way forward is unclear.

**AQ:** Yes, so let us start again. When you were observer consciousness, you felt that experience was very different from your earth one. Primarily, you felt as if you had no particular will. You could see the earth consciousness and programs as energies. That's because an observer energy/program doesn't need to be tainted. The observer energy is an aspect of my consciousness in a similar way your subconscious programs are to you.

You cannot make these and higher observations like I can, because your program has no parameters for such a focus. You are not denied, you are welcome, but the information required would be inaccessible to you because you would still see it through your intact earth programs.

**R:** That seems to be a common repeating theme!

**AQ:** Yes, vibrational compatibility. Let us come back to my observation of your thought, *Where does Robert's consciousness go on death?* My reply would be, "Where ever you wish, within your focus of vibrational compatibility."

The current understanding of your world is that when you leave your earth body, some might encounter energetic icons pertinent to their beliefs during their transition. Many expect to be greeted by old relatives and friends. But that transition realm, like earth, has levels within levels where like attracts. Those with caustic thoughts would exist alongside similar people to learn and, hopefully, vibrate a little faster with more love and understanding.

What initial levels you vibrate at or advance to will give the experience of *thought creation and desire gratification.* These are similar to earth desires, except they can be fulfilled because anything can be created by you. On earth, many did not see what they were creating or fulfilling. Some people will engorge and indulge themselves with unlimited opportunity for gratification.

There are no drugs, only energies to be used with love and skill. Drugs are an earth way of using chemicals to temporarily detach consciousness from the human body. If someone gets 'high' it is an experience of his or her higher vibrational levels. Any demons they experience upon return are their negative constructs seen within their own subconscious and psyche. Don't forget, chemicals have an energetic vibration, which interacts with the vibrations of the mind and body. Desensitising addictive behaviours here is a separate matter.

After a short period in transition, consciousness will adjust, and those who exercised choice to over indulge begin to see that none of that matters. Not only would it fail to make them feel good but would make them feel ill at the outcomes. It is rare, but some do not process this if they have a distorted compass.

In general, you become more aware of your thoughts and are able to observe them. The energy you create can become conscious and act on your behalf. The way of thinking is seen and you can energise different thought programs.

Guidance is always available from more evolved beings. They can explore with you the opportunities to alter the energies you created in previous lives. You would be shown timelines of possibility and how they interact with others. Parents will be mutually chosen as they in tandem choose children. These are the ways you can have the energy and DNA that you wish to experience.

And so life experience begins again. As a baby begins to grow, there may be adverse human feelings and sometimes a struggle to let go of who it was before. At times, the negative energies of the earth are too difficult to manage, or there has been a plan mutually agreed for the experience of bereavement. At those times, the soul has free choice and does not have to proceed with its birth.

When born, the baby begins to fill with more and more consciousness. There are several points of consciousness transition, but there comes a point when the required amount passes beyond the veil of forgetfulness. In this way, you have a different experience of believing you are someone else. And so this type of life goes on unless you wish to seek higher levels of light – and that is another matter.

A few humans think they have the veil removed because they have memories of lives on other planets, but that is memory program. We can choose to remember whatever we wish but only if it was part of the prepared timeline. It gives an experience of memory, which may take them on a personal discovery or to other planned experiences. If you existed aside from the earth collective consciousness and veil program, the additional stimuli would be substantial and life compatibility would not be, as you know it.

While you inhabit your earth body, you may learn or know that it is only a projection from yourself. You cannot feel it in the way that I do outside of your construct. If you did, you would be thinking and feeling like me. You would see the projection of yourself and be happy with whatever it was experiencing. You would be happy that you had allowed it the illusion of being separate. That is how I feel – my vibration is not compatible with living in the form you take.

All of our energies are connected, so responsibility for the energy we create is very important. It cannot be destroyed but it can be converted to something else – not necessarily through karma as per previous comments.

*(Turning and looking at me Aqueena says)*

You are not Robert he is a temporary experience – you are a part of my consciousness – I am allowing you to think you are separate. All of these things create such a wide variety of experiences. At the moment you are creating energy through thought and deed upon a timeline alongside others. Evolution is the ability to change the energy created by soul experiences.

When you return here you will see very quickly that you were an energetic projection into a life force. You will see what impact you had made on previous energetic projections.

Accepting the energies of past creation does not need to mean suffering. Orlacka previously told you how she lives and experiences her dimension. She will expand upon the life that she lives in order to explore different ways of working with energy.

**R:** Thank you.

**AQ:** I am welcome!

# FOUR

Orlacka is an Arcturian and she starts the dialogue by introducing us to the relationship of energy and form (including her appearance). She explains how restrictive energies exist in the mental space between the current us and the future us beyond transition.

 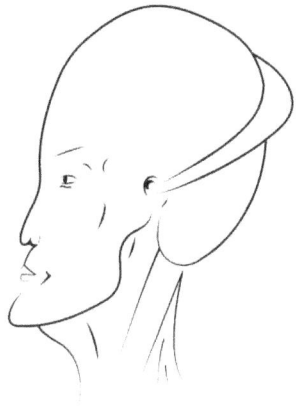

*Painting of Orlacka and profile sketch by Robert Lomax*

**Orlacka**: Hello my dearest boy, I can see all is well with you.
**Robert**: It's been a while since I've been called a boy!

**O:** Yes that statement was relative to my perspective and focus. As to my age and appearance, readers may find that somewhat unusual – so best I begin with that. Robert has shown several overlays of energy in the coloured painting. As you will realise by now, energy can take form, but it doesn't have to. For me energy and form are interchangeable. In this way, you can see several aspects of me in the same space. There are different levels of light and vibration around my head, which are active in several dimensions.

In profile, Robert has shown these energies, which look like fleshy projections around my head connecting to where you would expect my ears to be but again this is an energy function. I am a ninth-density being but that description is meaningless without context. Your third-density world has what you describe as dimensions of width, height and depth, plus time, but these four measurements do not make it fourth dimensional. I would describe dimensions as vibrational realities that have differing base programs. You appear to live in your program dimension, but you are also able to 'access' others with your present awake consciousness as well as your unconscious. Each of these reality programs, or dimensions, has a function more related to a way of being or thinking.

As your energetic vibration or 'light' becomes finer, you are more able to resonate with other densities or dimensions. You can reach higher dimensions when meditating, but you may not necessarily have full awareness or compatibility. Your soul already exists upon those dimensions. What you might begin to appreciate is that the representation of your soul upon those vibrations may look less like you than you might have thought. We have been challenging your concepts of what you believe you are and the way you think. The soul has a very wide spectrum of existence – Robert and I are aspects of an expression of our soul.

Not everyone involved in communication with Robert is an aspect of our soul. A pertinent example of this theme is Oritie. He is one of the 'key sweepers' between the third and fifth dimensions. It sounds a very grand title but it's just a role. He and other light beings are helping to sweep or refine humanity's consciousness in the zones between those densities. What exists between the zones can be seen in all manner of ways, depending upon the database of the viewer. The viewer can create distortions within them. The distance of the zones could be miles, or the blink of an eye as if it never existed as a partition. If there were no concept of partition or resistance, there would be none. There is nothing to keep you away from higher densities – only vibration and what you believe or fear.

Part of Oritie's role involves changing a few concepts of transition. The uplift will be very swift, but the mind could make the experience more difficult than need be. That, of course, depends upon the way the mind views the change. These I would describe as potential energetic mental resistances. These levels of mind are not constrained by time, so the concept of difference or change can create energy or occupy more space than need be, just by being aware of it. There are levels of sweeping or clearance that involve angelic and higher dimensional light beings as well.

Concepts of duality can interfere with the transition as you can see from the following. *Do you want to change to be different? What are you going to lose? What is the way and how do you get to the other side? Is this your decision because it feels as if it's happening without involvement? Do you have no choice? How can you be something if you don't know what you are to be? If you have no control, will you feel out of control?*

Unconscious programs work incredibly fast – in an instant, like a very fast computer. It is these programs and your interpretation or thinking about such programs that appear as time.

**R:** Did I hear correctly?

**O:** Yes, that is one of the reasons but it is also to do with the vibrational nature of your realm alongside the appearance of separation. It's all part of that level of the program. The transition will be instantaneous, but your experience of it will relate to the energy you use to interpret it. It will be quick and easy because the greater part of your life force knows what is to come. It has been waiting for the change because a part of you is already there. There will be many energies and forces involved with such a change. These will be on a cosmic level as well as your collective consciousness, which will be 'flipped'. Those with less light, who are willing to be a part of the change, will flow with the rest.

There have been many alien and human preparations working in tandem for this cosmic event. Concepts of *resistance* or *acceptance of change* are not required because they are two sides of duality or paradox. One cannot exist without the other, which is why sweeping and clearing by light beings is carried out. The transition will energetically charge the conceptual boundaries between these dimensions so that they become irrelevant or complete. In this way, one becomes the other with nothing in between – instantaneous vibrational upgrade for all things on the planet. Third-density will no longer be energised.

Common sense might suggest it would be helpful to understand and know the differences between these densities?

Wrong!

**R:** Pardon! I thought it would have been wise to let people know what to expect or what is different about the densities. Already many spiritual investigators and psychics have given guidance on the differences.

**O:** Is that using their database or copying and embellishing what someone else has said? Expectation creates a preformed idea of what will be received. You need to remember how powerful the mind is and what it creates or interprets. What I have said appears to be counter-intuitive to discovery through discernment.

**R:** But the mind will be changed or the way of thinking will.

**O:** These anticipations are in advance of the event and are part of your current database perspectives. There is no need to project current perspective upon the new. Those trying to keep their old programs after the change will remain in fourth density for longer. The idea is to have as many functioning in fifth-density as soon as possible. The fourth is transitional and different from the initial upgrade that Oritie and other sweepers are working on. I said counter-intuitive because, in some ways, actually talking about the uplift creates an expectation of certain things.

**R:** But if more people know about it, it will help to bring it into reality because of the mass-mind effect. What we believe comes into existence.

**O:** That is true but as I said earlier your database will constrain the energies as to what could form.

**R:** I see what you are saying, but can you say something that won't create pre-thoughts and distort the energies?

**O:** Well, let's put things into a different context. We can start from another reality, which is that each person's consciousness already exists in those dimensions.

**R:** If they follow through previous discussions, that consciousness is also energy with the appearance of body form, it might cause difficulty. It will not be easy if they are concerned that they exist 'in form' there.

**O:** Well they don't need to worry because they won't look like me or anyone else. Some of their consciousness exists there, but how much there is makes a difference to the amount of manifestation. For the main, this will be energetic – you are hung up on form as being someone else or seeing a physical doppelganger.

As consciousness upgrades, the human body will also follow. Let us describe them as energetic blueprints that already exist there. These will become more alive and because they are part of the new body information program – so the body will transform as well. You effectively become who you are programmed to be. I could omit the description 'transition' and say 'inevitability'.

Or I could say, "You will just remember what you already are and how you already exist at that vibration." These vibrational programs are being filled with more light energy all the time but are still in part dependent upon the activity of human consciousness. I could also say, "It's something that's already happened because you are already there, and it's more a question of shedding a shell than getting a new one."

**R:** Okay, I understand; the variety of our expressions correlates to the human paradoxical nature. But I also get the definite, the unquestionable, the no-doubt element of what is to be because it already exists at some level. However, people will still want to know the attributes of the different dimensions or densities.

**O:** Take time to reflect on what I have said. Do I need to say what is to be?

**R:** Well, it's a bit like intending to give a proclamation and then withholding what you know.

**O:** I don't think so.

**R:** I can't accept that – you know the difference between the way you and I exist, and you explain them as best as I can receive them.

**O:** But we are the same.

**R:** Clearly not in looks or the way we think.

**O:** I shall try a different tack then. You are looking at difference-making comparisons and evaluations. These you are processing through your database. It may be a database with a degree of understanding about the topic I speak of, but nonetheless, that is what you are doing.

**R:** I am just asking for you to explain the differences between the vibrational densities.

**O:** And I am trying not to show divergence because it is better for people to be calm and accepting and see that the universe is them. Otherwise, it's easier not knowing about the change at all because of the influence of database pre-thoughts and fears. People will still be themselves, but they will have an enhanced 'knowing' and they will feel more loving and less judgemental.

Earlier in the book, we said of timelines: "When you move on to a new one, your past seems to alter to configure with your present." We were showing you a concept of timelines and dimensions with the 'shimmering'. On the horse, the timeline initially appeared straight, but it jumped about to different positions. This was imperceptible to you and the way you live your life.

Before we finish this book, we will introduce other ways to see timeline concepts. That will give a greater understanding, which will be more compatible with the totality of what we wish to impart. I remind you that all has been planned with these presentations and all information is in an order to help you best understand. All you need do, Robert is to type what we say and sketch what you see.

We do not wish to follow other people's explanations and descriptions of the vibrational densities. We wish to provide other insights and ways of looking at them.

**R:** Very well, I shall follow your lead.

**O:** When the uplift takes place, it will be a bigger shimmer than the timeline shimmers you constantly undertake at the moment. It will be as if it had always been that way because you will be in that consciousness on the new timeline.

**R:** So did that timeline always exist, and was it just a matter of getting on to it? If it already existed, did it have a different origin? If that's my logic then the same must apply to all of them, even the small shimmers in our daily lives.

**O:** Some good observations and interesting questions: these shimmers are part of the infinite possibility of the Isness and the ability to change direction. If an alcoholic gives up the drink, he moves on to a different timeline, and the potential timelines as a drunk do not then get used.

**R:** But he will still have the memories of his past life, in contrast to what you were saying.

**O:** Memories and memory timelines are different. What you refer to is a memory, which flows with the timeline. In the case of the now teetotaller, his memory will appear to be a straight line back, even though it isn't. I am talking about memory programs of timelines and what actually needs to be remembered.

The uplift will create a big evolution; there will be memories that you did not have before. You will be able to access them in preference to the prior memories. The updated memories will be cognisant to the new experience.

**R:** I notice you are using specific words, which are coming to me more slowly. I need to look up 'cognisant' in the dictionary (it means having knowledge or awareness of); so did they exist as memories that can now be accessed?

**O:** Not in the way you think. In this new consciousness, you will have a different database. Much of the old ways of how to think will not be there either. You will think and feel in different ways, therefore you will interpret your database in new ways.

In addition, your database will have been upgraded as well. You will have a different way of interpreting different information. That will change memories because you will have different ways of interpreting your memories and the information about them will also be changed.

So, it's not a memory that was formed on another timeline, but it is your total adjustment or transformation to a new vibrational density. All things, including memory, adjust to it.

**R:** But will my old life be forgotten?

**O:** Do you want to remember it?

**R:** I'm not sure. At the moment it feels like a loss because those experiences made me who I am. So who am I without them?

**O:** That is part of the reason why Oritie and others have been working in the void, disentangling the concepts of loss and loss of self.

These are very powerful thoughts and they exist as a very necessary part of the self-protection programme in your current consciousness. What is the point of a memory?

**R:** I suppose, to define the self. I have other life memories, but they feel so far back they don't seem to define me now.

**O:** I would say you remember what you need to.

**R:** You mean *access* what I need to, as some sort of specific program for the memory?

**O:** Excellent, I could not have put it better myself – though, in fairness, that is what I am doing! As our minds become closer, you access me as I access you. This appropriately returns us to the point raised by Antemedi: "What is an original thought?"

Nothing is lost, as such; it's a matter of what light or energy you keep in which memories. This is not the same as the residual energies you created by doing things.

Why do you need to access all of the past?

**R:** Sorry to alter course, I just had a thought and if I don't ask I might forget. What about all the history books?

**O:** Ah, history, now that's different from memory. Historians are constantly rewriting history as they uncover new information and see events from different perspectives. As you know, histories are written by the victors, not the vanquished. Point taken though!

You will see what's written through the new way of thinking and disseminate it through a different database, which will change the outlook on written material. You will see falsehoods and the reasons why people have said particular things. In that way, the perception of history becomes undone.

However, it is possible for wording, objects or people not to be there on a new timeline. It will be hard to remember or know those people who were there before because they would be proceeding on a different timeline. Furthermore, your memory timeline program will have altered to suit your new circumstances. That's the way it's programmed for you on that level, although my memory programs work in different ways to that.

**R:** That's an incredible program!

**O:** It's one of millions – the soul is incredible.

**R:** So, with some people and things not being on the new timeline, you are talking about something quite radical.

**O:** Yes and no. It depends on why that timeline of omissions came about and what was intended to be created by their omission. Let's say, with counselling and confrontation of fears, a person can overcome PTSD. The energy of that event can be changed but not necessarily the memory.

Stress is often perceived as a memory that forces itself upon the victim – however, the energy of the actual experience is accessed through memory to process it. But, the processing of the energy doesn't always happen, because it's difficult to process it through duality in the subconscious.

So, to define further, it is the mind that accesses the specific past experience or trauma. It's not in this moment, but it is allowed in and recreated because it's attached to an event. It is the energies of the initial experiences. These are the residual energies created by yourself or others. This energy can be transmuted by changing it to another form – or by no longer needing to hold it for whatever reason. Those may include blame and guilt or apparent bad luck. In the section about healing, Arksar gave an example of how residual energies can be given back to the perpetrator and that is one way of healing PTSD on an energetic level.

If people are moved on to another timeline, they can still have residual created energy from the previous ones. They can undertake the work to heal it, or their higher self could remove it so that it can be dealt with at some later stage in different or easier circumstances. It depends on the experiences they require on the new timeline. Remember you are all constantly 'shimmering' anyway.

If any of you are moved to a timeline where you cannot access that memory you won't be able to access the residual energy through the memory. You may still have the energy and not be fully aware of its influence. Alternatively, you may have unknown feelings and no record of why they are there. Your science does not currently accept that energy created in a past life can affect you, particularly when hidden by a forgetfulness program. Perfect examples of this are the times when Antemedi took Robert back to over ten recent past lives, not all on earth. He was helped to transmute the energy he created. In one, he murdered his master during a period of the Roman Empire and in another, he suffered as a beleaguered and beaten slave. The reason he was given access to these memories was so that he could fully connect with how the negative energies were created and transmute them to positive energies. This happens when there is a willingness to take responsibility for energy in any or all lifetimes.

After the uplift, some may live the remainder of the new life with a changed memory access program. This means they will not have to feel the angst and terrors associated with past trauma. Each higher self can decide what is best to experience in their life.

**R:** Could hypnosis work?

**O:** In part, but the residual energy would have to be dealt with properly at some stage. Some timelines will have no access at all to trauma energy. Each to their own choice, as I just said.

The new uplifted levels will be changed so that cause and effect will be more instantaneous. People will be very aware of their thoughts and actions. There will be no need to suffer in order to learn, though it's not the end of suffering. In any case, suffering needs redefinition and understanding. You will not need to suffer to transmute energy. Who says there has to be suffering? 'There has to be suffering' is one of your programs that will fall by the wayside.

Anyway, back to my point about why a timeline means something is removed or forgotten. That said, in the cases I have spoken about, people would not have the awareness to know about the forgetting or program removal.

To understand more, you all need to consider the questions:

*Why is the timeline being created by your higher consciousness?* and *What is it creating for you to experience next, by removing what was before?* Maybe the answer is that nothing more can be gained from the previous types of experience.

At present, your experiences are constantly changing. They are part of self-aware programs of soul consciousness, but you don't experience them as changing. You're still on the horse going in a straight line.

**R:** An absolutely fantastic playground of choices. We have set the parameters for a program, but we can change it to a different game.

**O:** Within degrees. Sometimes individuals have directly interfered with an earth-common timeline of many people. It can rectify itself or its direction be returned. That can be monitored and interventions put in place to stop that. There are programs that cover this.

**R:** How do you undertake interventions if by doing so alters a timeline.

**O:** Ah, but we do, as part of other programs. I will review, but my answer will be different from the sponsoring thought of your question. Yours had the parameters of thinking that there is a correct timeline!

We are going into a subject area that you might find extremely obtuse or hard to believe. I can see you have a program constraint that says if information appears hard to believe, you will only follow it so far.

**R:** Okay, I will try to accept without interjecting.

**O:** Return to the previous images of the horse and the multitude of choices, namely the small, golden nuggets. The energy of these programs flashes and creates the shimmering from one timeline to another. If you look at the plane above, you can see similar zigzag movements, but not in the same places or directions. We already said that at higher dimensions of your soul, we have our own lives as well as the programs that interact with you.

Excuse me for a moment, I can see reverberations going much further afield. In the future, more people will find difficulty with the word 'program' than I anticipated. I thought my previous explanation might carry it through. Even if I use my word 'arkarna', that doesn't complete the gap in the bridge.

Much has been said about these interactive self-aware thought processes, but I'm only able to use your word 'program' to come close to my concepts. I could have said 'love programs', but that doesn't cover the complicated interactions and the lives being experienced. If we join them together as 'arkarna programs', then we will have a shared commonality and broader, more-encompassing description. I can see that sits much better.

Now then, what we have said so far has been quite matter-of-fact with direction and pace – we knew what you were to type and in what order. That is also part of an arkarna program. But what you have just seen, is me questioning an initial assessment of using the word 'program'. The 'excuse me for a moment' was an interruption to that flow, an apparent change to what was planned. We could say that it's an alteration to the timeline. Perhaps I am just showing you the ability to change my mind and giving you the experience of seeing me do it.

But was it always planned like that and, if so, what is its part in the overall creation of this presentation? Is it one of those thoughts or all of them? Has it interrupted the deeper explanation I was to give on the nuggets and the shimmering?

What we have in effect just done is to look at one of these energetic nuggets or programs. It seems as if we have slowed the whole process down by looking at one particular part of the arkarna program. It is our focus and what we are focused upon.

In many ways this is how you can experience life – it is a matter of focus as you question what you do. That's why you create another shimmer and another route; constantly changing focus points and observations all from different thoughts within you. We could say you have millions of energy points of observation. It is a matter of which one you are drawn to, as much as which choices or observation points are placed near to you. You may choose any one of them, but the one that would be more helpful to your evolution is always closest to you.

Even if you don't choose it, it is there in the next moment in another form. This is the arkarna program guiding you. It is self-adapting and it has awareness; it is part of the soul in the wider sense.

**R:** That doesn't seem obtuse.

**O:** Hold on to your socks! In the same metaphor, you and I can be side by side. We can walk forward in front of the horse. If you had a pair of white fluffy socks and the ground was sticky, tiny fibres would be left behind. We could see these as residual energies created by our choices and deeds. Perhaps every so often you might leave the old socks and change to a thicker pair in another colour with more fibre. In this way, you will deposit larger chunks of energy. Some of this energy could be an individual action, like the murder we spoke of, or a cumulative experience such as the slave in the quarry.

Energy at times sticks in clumps because like attracts like. Not all of it is negative, as it intermingles with loving energy. This can return to you in some form further down your timeline as part of cause and effect. Some of the negative

117

energy that returns as cause and effect can help growth through a negative experience. We need to leave judgement out of this explanation because good or bad deeds will hinder us. It was mentioned earlier that you could return in time to alter the energies of a timeline, so let's explore that.

A sponsoring thought informed by your database creates an action and becomes creative energy, which leaves behind residual energies. Energy cannot be destroyed once created – it can only be transmuted. That which you create remains until you change it. It affects you and informs your experiences on your timelines, which are also part of your arkarna and those around you.

I am you and you are the embodiment of me returning in time to change the energies I created on my timeline. That will bring in some unusual thoughts!

It could mean I have sent back a projection of myself and I am talking to it (you) from the future or another timeline. You think the problem with that is as follows: Orlacka is what she is now because of what she experienced. Therefore, if she went back in time, it would change who she is now. So – did you have a life without my interjection, or is this a repeat life with me now coming back to it?

It's not so much altering the timelines but transmuting the residual energies on them.

Unfortunately, that does not correlate with the life you live and the way you live it. Our consciousness is so diverse that you are experiencing an apparent 'future you' talking to you and changing your present outlook. But surely all of that is part of the timeline experience anyway – because it's a timeline that can be changed.

One of your other thoughts is that I have either come back to speak to myself or I have somehow moved on without your part of my consciousness.

**R:** Yes, very obtuse now, and blowing the socks off hasn't made this understandable.

**O:** Going back to the metaphor, we can see that the timelines or arkarna programs on other dimensions, above and below, have different directions and different life expressions as well as experiences. In order for all this to be compatible, you feel it has to be a program of different programs, with one being an over-arching program, even though the programs can change.

In this lifetime, you have changed some of the residual energies you created in previous lifetimes. Those residual energies were, in part, informing this lifetime experience. Such as when you were the slave: *It doesn't matter if I plead, argue or barter, I will never get my own way, so what I think or do has no matter or effect.* Those were some of the base programs that you were living early in your life as Robert. But you changed the energy of them on the level that they were created. You met and challenged those people and those old experiences on the 'same-level current consciousness'. Consequently, those thoughts no longer have energy within to inform your subconscious programs.

**R:** Perhaps you could have just changed it more easily with your greater wisdom and energy.

**O:** Well I did, through you. Like needs to meet like – acid needs an alkali to neutralise it. Wise words by themselves are insufficient and the energy you are changing does not vibrate at my level for 'like to like'. That 'hurt and damaged energy' existed at your level and had to be dealt with there, by facing up to those deep feelings and changing them.

You needed to fully accept the hurt as an experience and not as a reason to continue suffering. Self-appraisal and wisdom were insufficient and you needed to experience giving back the injustice and pervasive negative energy to the perpetrators.

This is the responsibility to heal yourself and regulate the negative energy you created. When you do this, it will feel like good energy flowing back to you. But it doesn't, it's your energy, it was always with you because you created it and it belongs to you. It's about accepting that you are the totality of your energy. *It or you* reside in the dimension in which you created it. It's up to you to decide what to do with it.

**R:** I can feel the deeper meaning of that now. Previously, I would have not seen it as my energy or your deeper definition of me. While it is transmuting energy, I can more fully see I am transmuting myself.

Thank you, my responsibility is accepted, and I am grateful to those of me who have helped. I can see the relevance of repeating themes because when they are explained in new ways it gives different meanings.

But how does this tie in with the 'obtuse' changing the past residual energies without affecting the future self? And, of course, how Robert's life fits into this?

**O:** Indeed, let us become obtuse. I shall show you some unconscious thoughts. *As much as I try, I can't see the way forward – frustration gets in the way and makes me more frustrated. Because there seems to be no answer, there is only one choice, which is to carry on doing the same until things change, even though it feels they won't.*

This is both about knowing and not knowing what it is possible to know. You have your frustrations, which you are placing at my feet. It is not for me to solve your frustrations. I thought you had agreed you would be responsible for the energy you created.

**R:** Ouch! That is true, but I was expecting you to unfold something more interesting or incisive.

**O:** You think this is not incisive because you don't understand.

**R:** Ouch again! But isn't it your responsibility to give guidance through this process?

**O:** I am, but you are interpreting me through frustration. If we agreed to say you need nothing, no more wisdom and no more insight, then we can stop this dialogue here and say nothing further.

**R:** Then that would be pointless I would be rather marooned.

**O:** I want to take you towards true pointlessness. No worth, no reasoning, no way forward or back, nothing to change. No growth, no evolution – a beautiful world but nothing of any value to you. Again we bring you to the same doorway, and you place yet another value on its threshold.

**R:** But did we have to go through all the above just to say "let's go past the threshold of value again"?

**O:** Well that was dependent upon your hope, anticipation and expectations, which you needed to give up as they affected your value systems.

**R:** Yes, thank you – that was my frustration at having expectations deflated or not fulfilled. But for a book entitled Communication and the Alien Mind, we seem to have gone off-piste a little.

**O:** That's your perspective. I repeat earlier thoughts, *The alien mind is unknown to you, and your mind is also alien because it is unknown to you.* Take a moment and we will deal with this energy.

**R:** *(After a short while spent releasing these programs energetically with Orlacka, I return)*

**O:** Value has no efficacy, it is not a consideration – love exists but not in the way you think or anticipate. We have repeated that often to you for good reason. Arksar talked of the Mowhar paradox and this in part defines your approach to the subject. There is nothing to value in these realms, that's why you couldn't proceed because you were filled with anticipation and hope. You did not know what you could hope for.

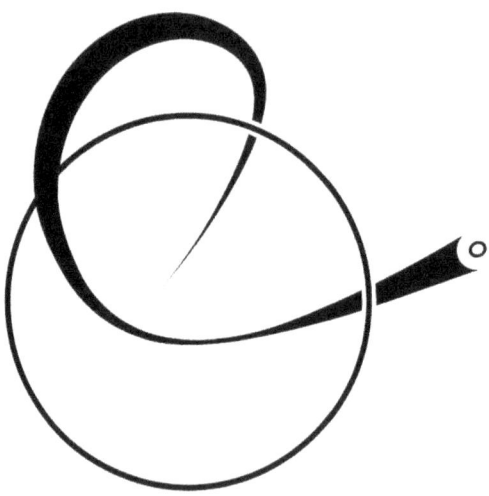

*The symbol for Mowhar, the never-ending circle*

*Arksar pops in and he draws a circle with a line looping in and then back out.*
He says, "This is our symbol for Mowhar, the never-ending circle – all things as one. Within the sphere, you begin to experience all that is paradox, but you do not fully know it. When you know it for what it is, you can exit with that knowledge. You then enter nothing and you don't know what to do. You are not prepared for it because 'you are unknowing of anything else' at that level. So, you may re-enter paradox

122

from nothing, but this time you know what you will encounter.

"As you do, you realise that Mowhar holds nothing more than a different version of the same and you can't go back to what you were – learning Mowhar would be repetition. If you now exit her, you do so knowing there is nothing more she can give to you and you have no reason to return. At this point, you can be free of Mowhar even when you work within a collective consciousness that is attached to it.

"Nothingness is *only the barrier* formed on the outer edges of paradox because paradox was born in nothingness. It is a symbol and it signifies 'that which was' now holds nothing of relevance to different ways of being."

*At this point, Arksar fades away.*

**O:** Let us return to the previous metaphor of the horse and its journey. It has connections with the symbol supplied by Arksar because we shall be returning to a previous understanding – but with a very different outlook.

As we enter the metaphor, you may move around freely and experience it. When you were previously riding the horse, you felt you were experiencing life because you were so immersed in it. You also experienced higher level observing, which felt dispassionate and quizzical. So what I now propose is that we shall join these two aspects together.

You and the readers of this article might think you live life and you observe it. That's your sense of it in your way of thinking and you hold to this. We have shown you that your thinking can blind you and that's why our ways of observing seemed so unusual.

**R:** You haven't fully shown your way of thinking yet!

**O:** I am aware of that. But back to my delivery. You create an action which you then experience and, if you wish, you can reflect upon your deeds. This is observation in arrears. When you think about what you want to do, it is database driven but duality constrained. So your observation in arrears is limited to database and duality.

We are now entering the holographic metaphor on the higher plane where we can observe without those constraints. Previously, as an observer, you felt detached from expectation, desires and hopes, perhaps even humanity itself.

That my dear soul counterpart (Robert) is actually much closer to clear viewing than you have ever been before and far more perceptive than what you can see with your eyes. It does not filter, direct or set parameters from any database. The observation pays no value to your current thoughts. Not only do the thoughts have no value but they are also valueless in a place that does not see from those constraints. The parameters of love are different as well.

Because this is such a long way from the way you think, it seems unfathomable. You feel it is a major reduction in your senses. But here loss cannot exist and neither can gain. Love cannot be lost nor regained; it cannot be ascribed or described, so it is very different from your human feel of it. That does not mean it has less worth than your love because you do not understand or feel it in the same way. There is neither suffering nor can there be an escape from suffering – nothing to be uplifted from and there is nothing to aspire to. No wonder you struggled again at the threshold.

So how can I place context upon this place and give a sense of what it is like for me? We are not talking at cross-purposes but about very alien experiences to the ones you currently process.

As observer, you are at a much higher dimensional vibration, so we must proceed with descriptive caution. More so than before because you can only partially understand who

I am and what is possible. It is all good news if you are to put a measure upon it. I can say that to you, and its effect on you is neither good nor less good. Arkarna love is much more diverse than you could imagine.

If I were to say that I love Robert unconditionally, it simply means with no preconditions. But it's not the same kind of love that you are used to (feeling good by the giving and receiving or being uplifted). While there are higher dimensions than this, if I go there I am not uplifted nor do I have no more worth or love. I choose the consistency of my words so that they act as a mirror reflecting back your own values.

So let me begin to show you from here what is here. Your phrase would be: 'Walk a mile in someone else's shoes to know them.'

For this next exercise, let us all stand at the last shimmer of your current knowledge. We are aware that our lives proceed and we live on several dimensions. But as we enter this particular program, we can all move forward in unison. We all take a step at the same time and in that program and this moment we are at one, we are the same. While we are 'one and the same', our experience of that depends upon the arkarna program that we exist in.

It is easier to see dimensional programs without earthly constraints, so we will go even further than your previous heightened observer experience. As you take a deep breath, suck and draw energy through the top of your head. On the out-breath, push it out through your feet. You will begin to feel yourself rising upwards (**R:** this is known as fluting). You can look down at where you came from, but be aware of the new vibrations we have reached. We have left the reflective mirrors to the lower dimensions.

Brighter beings – light in the shape of human bodies come towards us. Different arkarna programs mean that timelines

125

exist, but they are more fluid – changing with every footstep we take. There are no nearby choices or patterns to follow as the next best. The layers of golden threads fold over one another. Let yourself be surrounded by these souls and feel their presence. They have peace and gentility, they are curious and have no fear, shame or mistrust. They are trusting but they are not ignorant to the point that innocence makes them vulnerable. They cannot be offended by your reactions – they are free from that.

I can see you are so overwhelmed by their purity and love that you have failed to detect their great wisdom and power. Your world does not often see compatibility between the two.

**R:** *(Orlacka is elaborating on my feelings she is explaining what I am feeling – it's as if she is me talking)*

**O:** As we follow these beings, you can see that they produce golden threads as they walk. These are the places we were all due to walk today. Even our threaded path intermingles with theirs.

Gulwah is the name of the person I would like to introduce you to.

**Gulwah (G):** Welcome to you all – I say that because I know and understand there is a wider audience. I am aware of the need to be precise.

What you have been shown by Orlacka are metaphorical interpretations. These have been specifically prepared so that you may understand certain concepts. You will still see these in your reference terms, so we would like to help you see them in ours. We haven't provided the full picture because we cannot provide the best explanation in your terms alone.

Obtuse was a word used earlier; perhaps 'a new field of vision unconstrained by current understandings' would be more helpful. Observation 'anew' in each moment without relationship to previous thoughts. There is nothing to hold to and nothing to compare to. It is a way of being and thinking and it is the way we think as Arcturians. Orlacka has been leading you here gently so you are more likely to feel what it's like to be at one with us.

After all, a deeper and more open way of sharing experiences is the best way to know someone else.

You have seen the limitations of your own *ways*. Your limits give you the experiences you require and desire but I do not judge what I observe.

Come closer to me and share with me at my vibrational observation.

**R:** I am connected to Gulwah, and I can feel so much unlimited love, there are literally no limitations to it, the energy is boundless. There is bounty for everything that we want to think and do in any program, but more can be accessed if needed. And yet, there is no need to do anything, which means discernment has no limitations. The self is selfless but all is well with that. There is great companionship within a compatible union; they embrace a love of all things. Events do not have our pain in them and there is a joy in expression and living. No grasping, no need, so desire and the decision-making process form naturally as part of the loving arkarna program. I was about to say arkarna at this level but he is showing me it's what they have all created to reflect who they are.

He says other races of beings on similar densities do not all think and act in exactly the same way as Arcturians, even though their vibrations are very similar. I wonder if it is their race's best expression of what it means to be Arcturian.

**G:** Of several expressions of Arcturian; we do not all appear the same. We do take on board other race experiences, particularly where we are inter-soul related. That is a form of loving responsibility for the energy at those other arkarna levels of soul.

**R:** Thank you for the correction. Being with you, there is a greater sense of creating and adapting your arkarna programs directly, then allowing the arkarna to work for you. Your program is a way of 'just being', your fluid consciousness does not need to gravitate to specific requirements. In fact, it is a program that requires you to have no specific requirements; parameters that exceed Mowhar and duality, if indeed they are parameters.

**G:** We have no requirements, we have no needs, we are not fixed as you say, and we are fluid thinking but also fluid with each other. We are not a hive, we are still individual, but we share a greater depth of thought. This works through our arkarna.

You have seen how your earth programs work. You program yourselves to believe you are free, but you still feel the need to escape because something is missing.

Your arkarna programs give you the information that accords with your way of being. If it gave you different information, you would be different beings. One is the other, and vice versa. It's a form of control and manipulation because you are programmed to believe you are free within it.

Your freedom is a sense of self-individualisation. In which case, some of you will sense our arkarna realm as non-individual because we share so much more in common.

That may be at odds with your ideas of freedom. Yet, you have your own commonality in a collective consciousness and a unified arkarna, so are you as individual as you believe you are? Like us, you also share with one another your thoughts and feelings, but yours is at your disclosure or comfort and to your program. Some of you think that others do not sense and know you fully because of individual autonomy. But they are blind in seeing that if they deny feelings and subconscious programs, they will leech out around themselves. They deny their own energy by not seeing that it is in common with one another.

We have no such discomfort and have nothing to hide because our subconscious thoughts are not constrained by limitations of duality and paradox – those are not active within us.

Yes, our way of being is far away from your way of being. Our joy and understanding may be unfathomable to you. For example, we have no compassion for you, only love. Compassion requires empathy to feel for you. We do not feel in the same ways so that is a big difference. To empathise, I would also need to feel as you feel in yourself and give consideration to your suffering. But we do not suffer. Why do we need to feel your suffering? That will not help you and that will not help us. We understand and we know the parameters of your arkarna, your way of thinking and being. To revert to your way of being will not help – only you can help yourselves. There is always guidance and choice and with the uplift, there is great opportunity to be different.

Our love works in a broader fashion, perhaps a bigger picture you might say, and we help in ways we are yet to explain. Discovering who we are is a process and one that is ongoing; it cannot happen within a few words of this book. Communication and understanding inter-dimensional beings is a massive undertaking because you so easily slip into seeing others from your perspective, not theirs. That is omnipresent with you; it is always there, that is the way you are it is your arkarna.

You might like to see reminders about your way of thinking being given to you more gently. But without rigorous challenges, you are more likely to be asleep to 'why you keep thinking like that'. So, I make no apologies for repeating observations when appropriate. It is said with love; but if it causes frustration or pain, that is your arkarna interpretation of my observation.

Our minds span dimensions in ways you could not imagine. Your vibrations have no effect on us unless we tune ourselves down to you. We scan and view in an objective way. We see things in terms of energetic production, thought and arkarna programs. We help you energetically with what we can but so often that is dissipated and overwhelmed by darkness in your collective consciousness.

We take part in an intergalactic presence and communicate with you alongside many others. Much of this work takes place on your higher vibrational levels. Agreements take place about what you wish to assimilate individually or collectively. It is not a matter of persuasion but showing possibility.

This responsibility is taken on under an umbrella of our type of love. We are also in part responsible for the energy you have generated. It's not a responsibility where we take yours away from you but to help and guide.

Orlacka spoke about going back to change the residual energy of an event where some of your energy has been distorted or damaged. Often, it can be healed permanently without needing to prolong the process. Rather than working backwards through a series of resultant energies in the form of recent events, the wound energies can be worked on directly by visiting the energy of past lives many times before. Not only do we heal and replenish the energies of the past, but we can also go back in time to when they took place and not only change the energy but the event.

Movement through time has already been mentioned and you wondered what effects that may have.

I will start by saying that time runs at different rates in

different parts of the universe. It can be slowed or stopped, be relevant or not exist. These functions are part of the arkarna programs, which are an extension of group consensus relative to each dimension. There are also different time periods in different parts of the universe, but that is my way of fitting information into your linear view that time always goes forwards.

We can relocate our selves into different periods – our vibration allows us to do that. We do not just heal the energies of the past, but we can alter choices made in the past or push one timeline on to another. This is usually where choices are ambivalent or where the wisdom to make an informed choice has not had the opportunity to energise.

**R:** All my previous questions still stand – if you alter your past, will it change your future now?

**G:** What if it's possible to alter your past without affecting the future. Orlacka said that part of the past timeline is that it would be altered.

**R:** So by altering it, you're not actually changing things because the alteration was due to happen?

**G:** Your awareness of what it means 'to alter' is rather limited. In the horse rider metaphor, you were initially unaware of the shimmers or the altering timelines.

**R:** OK, point taken; there is a constant shimmering on the lower timelines and we are unaware of the changes while in the experience. Whereas you are aware of them in a different way. But I can't see this correlates with manifesting in different portions of time.

**G:** You do that now. Where are your thoughts? You can spread them over the moment of now which contains past and future.

**R:** That is not putting myself back into a past event.

**G:** That is so, but I wanted to begin with the pliability of mind. By moving 'up in yourself' and above the earth self, you have been able to view your life and the shimmers it contains, be they past or future. In order to do that, you are not specifically located to yourself but within a collective mind/arkarna that is also pliable and not time dependant.

Look in front of you. I am showing you several parallel lines that represent the same life in the same space, but they are alternative lives of experience. Upgrade the metaphor to include the shimmers appearing all over the place. Rather than lots of possibilities laid out in one large plane, see instead energetic corridors with shimmers, which show the actual route. Take a moment to allow that into your mind.

Another way to grasp the concept is to see a corridor as a straight line but the floor moves or relocates within the corridor at each footstep and if you focus forwards you will not feel you are moving all over the place. Shimmers appear within the corridor and you are then on any possible timeline that the shimmers take you to – or take to you.

Our metaphor has changed slightly, but it had to be the way it was initially in order that you could get to this point right here in the now. There is no wrong metaphor, we give you only different ways that are useful. We could say that this metaphor is on a different timeline to the previous one.

**R:** That's stretching the information to fit the point you make.

**G:** That is because you are sceptical of what I am saying and the way I am overlaying information on the previous. As we get further along, you will see that what I have said now becomes superseded and just a part of the route to another realisation.

Concentrate – let us float up so you can look down on the

same corridors, which will now be below us in a slightly different way.

You will be able to see the resultant corridors walked. There are many of them because they now encompass different lifetimes and incarnations. By being outside of them we can see them in a different way.

**R:** The lives all seem to run in one direction and are concurrent, all happening on the same plane.

**G:** That will do as an explanation for the moment. From where we observe, we can put our focus into any one of these lives.

**R:** Yes I can feel and see some of those incarnations but it's not the same as going back into the past.

**G:** We are getting there! At the moment, we are presenting concurrent incarnation corridors with energetic edges, which do not obscure your view. The experience in the lifetime means the view within the 'corridor of energy' creates its own reflective environment. The life experience is restricted and contained to the one experience. We can literally focus on whichever one we wish at whatever point we wish. It matters not if you believe they are past or future.

Your only determination of past and future is how it relates to your particular point in time in your current life. What appears to be before it or afterwards is not relevant at our level. From the observer here you are seeing the energetic outlay of them all. They are all being lived energetically as programs.

**R:** But I can't be in all of them at every point in time.

**G:** It's all a matter of focus. Your original linear focus on the horse was towards the future in a straight line, but we have already shown that is an illusion and you jump on to different timelines through the shimmers. Time can be changed or made non-existent. It is only your focus and way of thinking that keeps it linear.

Focus back in the corridor where the shimmers happen and the floor moves or reappears in a different place. In this way, you can view timelines as constantly shifting. As you stand there, which portion of time do you think it would be?

**R:** Not sure it matters.

**G:** Good you can sense how that question has no importance or relevance to the observer. It's all a program that is shifting and then interpreted by you and your arkarna program to give you the experience you need.

**R:** OK, I can see why you are building this in layers – I hope no one reading this is lost!

**G:** Try to think of this all as arkarna. A constant evolving self-aware shifting program that is an extension of soul and part of the great pulse which is on all dimensions in different ways on each.

**R:** Wow! Now that's really interesting; the metaphor has disappeared and I can see human figures in the same place. They are all me and they are fluctuating as they stand there. I am watching the energy of them changing. They are flashing from child to adolescent to old man and back again, then repeating; but perhaps with just one minor alteration.

I get it – you're showing me that nothing is fixed including timelines, though there are some with more probabilities than others. The arkarna is constantly evolving. The program is constantly changing. Is it more a question of when we jump in to experience it? Do we do that when there are not many changes to make or when it fits in with other people?

**G:** You are picking up on me well but there are nuances still to grasp. It is possible to focus on any lifetime and in any order.

*R: (At this moment I have finished the book and I am checking for typos when I am thrust back into the metaphor to gain another perspective) We have all these lives at once but somehow the arkarna give us the experience of one lifetime at a time?*

*A: Yes, that's why you are also seeing the corridors or lifetimes now overlapping because they are crossing the same energy points. Each time, the energy at a shimmer can be revisited and changed; this is how you deal with resultant energies or karma. There is progression, which you see as linear, but it's actually just a series of overlays that keep changing. You are creating and changing resultant energies. At higher levels, you are already who you are; that's why Orlacka and Gulwah said changing the past doesn't change them.*

*R: It is so clever of you to put multiple meanings in this metaphor. I am inserting new information in this book that didn't happen when first constructed. It's an example of changing the resultant energies of the first typing – changing the book and some of its direction. What was said before is beginning to make more sense now; it's 'just a program', all I am is a bloody program – that's all Robert is. I am moving my focus about all of the time and rewriting timelines to alter resultant energies; what an incredible program – what an incredible consciousness to be able to do that. It's mind-boggling! At some level, this is all done but at the same time, it's still being created?*

*A: Yes Mowhar shows her creation everywhere, here and not here.*

*R: So, how are we going to get back to the book without altering its flow?*

*A: Well we have changed its timeline, so the way in which you continue with your typo checking will be changed. You will have another perspective in which to view what was said.*

*R: That means rephrasing some sections then?*

*A: Is that not an example of timelines constantly changing? Each one of us who took part in this book is available to you at any moment; we are part of its timeline.*

*So as you can see – you now have an answer to your previous question: "Does it mean that the alteration to a timeline is already known and*

135

*part of its timeline?" On one level it is complete, on another, it is being revised and revised. And between revisions, you can be aware of them being revised. It seems as if I have come from another version of our experience in the future to alter the current one and the past one because we will be altering some sections of the book.*

*R: So this is how you are a future version of me as is Orlacka but at another one, you are also both programs that our soul dips in and out of in its focus. That's how it continues to create.*

*A: Yes and no; that is only part of it.*

*R: Thank you, I was having the feeling that something was missing from this book and that the explanations were not full enough.*

*A: Everything for a reason.*

*R: So I just return to checking typos how is that going to work?*

*A: You will find out when you do; that's the point of an experience on a timeline that's constantly changing. Though now you have the experience and awareness of how it happens.*

*R: Thank you.*

*A: I am welcome.*

*G: Hello Robert, I see you are back. All the time you were checking for typos and making minor adjustments, we were with you in your thoughts helping you. That is after all the beauty of an arkarna program that is consciously aware. Perhaps you can use this additional fluidity that you now feel and allow things to unfold with ease.*

*R: Do we need to show what was in the previous book and what information has changed?*

*G: Does that really matter? That's part of what we are getting over to you. Constantly changing timelines and then revisiting them to change them again. It's all fluid.*

*R: I know who you are now. You are Gunther who gave me some of the initial information at the start of the first articles written for my website. At that stage, I was unaware of my soul connection to Arcturians and would have been challenged by your appearance and name as Gulwah. In the same way, I did not want to accept your appearance at my bedside when I was a young boy because I thought some of you were monsters and I was frightened.*

*G: And how did you know that information?*

*R: I just did – it was unwavering beyond all doubt – perhaps you helped by giving a nudge in my mind in the present.*

*G: All of those – the arkarna programs are most wonderful are they not?*

*R: Yes, magnificent. I feel more rounded on these subjects. Though a question, either from you or me, has formed in my mind, namely that this doesn't cover time travelling in a physical way from one moment to another.*

*G: That is also part of an arkarna program and another experience as part of the greater arkarna programs. I understand, however, that you would like to know the physical process behind that, even though it is part of the fluxing pulse.*

*R: Does going back to a past time on earth mean it has to be there in physical form?*

*G: That question shows that your pliability needs more refinement. Remember, it's all a program. It's a matter of focus; you dip in and out of your life constantly, but your experience of it in an arkarna program is one moment to the next. You think Robert's life is a constant flowing from one moment to the next when it is not.*

*R: So what about future telling and psychic viewing of future events.*

*G: You mean which version will you see, and why are you seeing the right version or the most likely in its revisions? Not forgetting that at another level it's already complete!*

*R: I partially see what you mean because I haven't grasped the fullness of it.*

*G: No but you will. However, I will not say when because that may spoil the unfolding. Arkarna programs are also meant to be enjoyed as an experience!*

*R: So we now just dive back into the reading for typos. I'm a bit concerned it won't make sense.*

*G: Ah! This intervention means it will make more sense. It also gives the feeling of fluid time to the readers; after all, the feeling of knowing is part of a way to the full knowing, i.e. 'just knowing'. They will know more easily and understand the older typing. They will experience it as a form of 'observing' the previous book. They have advance knowledge of what was not explained or gained by you at that time. They will see you trying to gain some concepts that they now hold. In any event, not all the information will be about the topic of fluid timelines.*
*R: OK, so the next typing of G for Gulwah is the previous typing.*
*G: Yes, let's see how it goes!*

**G:** The meaning of retrograde can be misunderstood – it refers to a lower density experience. It's not a lower-value experience, as we do not ascribe values to such differences.

This raises a point – what is a life experience if it can be different versions within the evolving arkarna program? Furthermore, it can be out of step from what you consider to be an order and not flow from one life to the next in date order.

**R:** This is mind-bending stuff, difficult to grasp and accept.

**G:** But you know there is truth in what I say, even if you do not see the whole picture.

**R:** I don't doubt what you say, and you are all bringing this story together in your own different ways. It would be easier to retreat into what I can understand because it is more comfortable. But I want to understand that which I can't.

**G:** You will not be able to understand some things because of the vibrational fields that you look from, but there is still a lot more that you can understand. I shall press on now because you have absorbed the new groundwork. It will add to a revolution in thought and a way of thinking.

**R:** You talked about movement between different lives and out of apparent order.

**G:** Yes – that fascinates humanity doesn't it? What if your focus could be in any of the lives and it wasn't restricted to one or another? What if one moment you are in Robert and in another moment you are Arksar or one of your other apparent past lives. What if you flit between them all – in and out of them?

**R:** Good grief! What a crazy life, as if you couldn't make up your mind where to be or what to do next. There has to be some over-arching arkarna program to all these lives. But it would mean lives last forever or as short or long as you wish. It's certainly not how I experience this life. This information is extremely obtuse; you have achieved what you said you would. It has no correlation to my life and its linear appearance.

**G:** That's as maybe.

**R:** You have said it's not travelling back into the past but it's travelling into different lives, which have "apparent flow in time". That is not time travel.

**G:** Not as you may think of it but we can I expand upon that at another stage. At the moment, I will say that technologies can be used to move about in time – to jump from one period physically to another, or to another place or location. That is not in the natural flow of timelines and shimmers and the arkarna levels of soul. There are also portals that exist which allow physical movement through non-space, but this moves the subject away from my explanations of arkarna.

We have been showing you many types of energy and different types of focus. Experience arkarnas – observing arkarnas – over-viewing or planning arkarnas – the ability to place a focus into different dimensional realities of life. A large gamut of possibilities and probabilities for expression.

**R:** Mind-boggling.

**G:** Yes, that could be your experience of it if you were not coached properly. I am placing a different energy above your crown chakra, which I would like you to pull through your head and push out through your feet. This will enable you to float into another more rarefied atmosphere. You are also attached to my vibration, so you may also focus through my thoughts and me. In that way, you will be able to interpret things which would otherwise be beyond your comprehension.

**R:** After taking in the energy, we both float together and enter an arena where there are humanoid beings walking from one side to the other.

**G:** Belenque – you know this Andromedan word means 'good', but you also understand it has a much deeper and more expansive meaning. Mowhar and arkarna programs are different from each other but, in a similar way to belenque, there are other depths to their realities.

This next experience will be one of those. You will experience it as an exchange. I remind you that everything is open to you and there is no limit to what you may experience. The rationale behind this particular arkarna is a free exchange of experience. It allows participants to show each other the energies they have experienced and what it is possible to experience. They can then see what the additional energies will do for them as individuals or for their group soul energy.

**R:** You have exceeded obtuse.

**G:** It may appear so. It's my way of showing soul interaction and connectedness. Soul knowledge and experience is shared but we view it as energetic resonance. You choose what resonance you wish to vibrate at or bring forth for the benefit of the soul group. It is an arkarna program that acts like a combined entity, which serves the soul groups. The arkarna is

140

a part of all that is here so participants may observe how altered resonances will function.

We previously referred to 'over-arching programs' and 'programs within programs', and we said by vibrating faster you will be in communication with higher aspects of the soul. When you do this, you will be more aware of your eleven other individuated parts of the higher self. This is not a sideways communication from you to them but through the higher self, which contains you all.

Each twelfth part can have as many experiences within different arkarnas as it wishes, even if they correlate or are very similar to the other eleven parts. These experiences programs are part of higher self arkarna, so with faster vibrations, you may access the general experiences and the 'program of learning'. Aqueena is the 'vibratory compilation' of the six female souls in your higher self and she is the half equivalent to the female/male entity higher self.

**R:** I thought that male and female twin flames united.

**G:** They can do but while they have individuated experiences they may access higher self in its most female or male expression because that's more comforting. So all-6 female individuated souls would see Aqueena as their higher self. This is a 'communication arkarna' so as well as being a program it is also a *way* of communicating. To see yourself in different guises or as different beings in different situations is a part of communication.

I am talking to you, but in order for this communication to work, you have to understand it within your earth arkarna and parameters. Some of the information is being processed through your mind and some through the physical brain. Good communication is about good understanding.

How you interpret these levels is down to our guidance and

141

a belenque (a good way) is to give you metaphorical constructs one upon another.

**R:** So what we see here isn't necessarily what is here?

**G:** Oh, yes it is – it can be anything if it gives you the understanding you need. What is really here? That is what you are thinking and it is all part of your conundrum.

The answer to that is arkarna soul connectedness and infinite possibility. In order for that to exist in that particular way, there has to be an infinite number of ways of seeing existence. If things 'exist and don't exist', ways of seeing them become more fluid.

**R:** Is there a consensus way of seeing?

**G:** Yes, there can be, but that is more to do with what you are comfortable with. A person from a strict religious background looking into the subject of soul connections might be happier with interpretations relative to their teachings rather than strange alien beings.

**R:** But once those constructs are gone and the database is not in gear, is there a consensus?

**G:** In terms of vibrations and the loving intent of communication – yes. The interplay is within the higher collective consciousness or arkarna of the higher self. Everyone has these channels of arkarna working in their daily lives. Most are unaware of them because that would serve them no purpose. It is a functioning, loving entity program, but it is also you and the joint souls within it.

Our more aware contact with it has a purpose. We understand its higher functional existence as well as the ability to communicate directly with it.

When you know what it can do, you can extend your use of it. It's not like shopping for what you want because these arkarnas respond to intent and action.

Higher self arkarnas will present themselves to you in order to correspond with the more personal arkarna programs you use. Conceptualising higher self, as a form of humanoid, is common; it can then be seen as the embodiment of the individuated souls. Please remember that, as an over-arching arkarna program, it is also you.

**R:** What other things can it teach or give us.

**G:** I am glad you did not say, "Can I ask it questions?" because the arkarna would reflect back to you your desire and reason of asking. Such questions born from your level of asking would meet you at your level, and you wouldn't learn much about them. This level of arkarna is functioning way above your needs and desires. Its awareness spans much further and includes lifetimes and timelines.

**R:** Explanations about the relationship of all these lives in the same moment of now seems a little lacking.

**G:** That is so – however understanding a little more about the arkarna higher self program is part of that explanation. Communication with this arkarna is more about what it has for you 'as itself' and what it 'gives to itself'.

It may sound strange to be communicating with a loving program that is self-aware, but it is a function of you – your interactive awareness. I am trying to show its vast capabilities and attributes. In truth it is not an 'it' nor is it a 'him/her' and your language limits explanation of its expansive nature. For your benefit, I will refer to this entity program as 'her'. Let us proceed further and see what she has to say to you.

*Higher self Arkarna program (**HSAP)** starts speaking*
**HSAP:** It is useful to see the difference between the embodiment of me and the function of me. Any part of me can have an interaction with me. It can be likened to your own

143

conscious programming that exists with you now and the experience of you being Robert. I am situated within you and without you. Non-locality is not a problem for me.

You have been learning about non-locality through metaphorical communication. You think there are some holes in the present information, so I can help with what you think.

Non-linear and non-time vibrational realities take you to some unusual concepts that are difficult to relate to your current experience. I start by reminding you that you are energy and your body exists within the pulse; it is 'there and not there'. Your mind is also non-local, but it is also compartmentalised in order that you may have many different experiences.

You now have a construct that your future and past lives are some kind of program that you dip in and out of. This is a comfortable way of seeing that energy format.

If I say that you are all these arkarna programs and they are alive at the same time, then every version of you in every moment would have to exist in the moment. To you, that seems nonsense because of your current experience. The inordinate amount of information and energy that's required to undertake such a thing is beyond your comprehension.

Orlacka explained about changing residual energies that you/we have created in the past. Dealing with those created energies sits comfortably with you.

In your current incarnation, you have experienced going back to previous lives to change residual energy. You have also visited the lives of others where you have directly intervened, making suggestions for changes to that life. This was done in conjunction with me as higher self arkarna. I presented the situations to you (my compartmentalised self) in order to have experience and change my/our residual energy.

In a similar way, interventions are happening to you at this

144

moment from outside the timeline that you are experiencing. This is how it is with all souls.

You experience linear time and a form of consciousness. It shows itself in your world as a constant, even though you are within pulse and connected to all that came from Mowhar. Your consciousness is inter-dimensional with apparent segregations. It is not with you all of the time. Your mind is in tune with other dimensions vibrating to their own specific pulse. Your focus is not inside your body in the constant way that you feel it. It is elsewhere.

I am you and you need not say, "where else is elsewhere?" because my answer would be *when else*.

Let us pull together these diverse understandings so they become cohesive. You have begun to accept that you are many forms of arkarna with a multitude of focus possibilities and different ways of communicating.

Time travel, as you see it, is to take your physicality out of your current world through non-time space in order to locate it in a different place and time. Your current body forms within your dimensional pulse; it is there by virtue of the information fields and the harmonies. It is and it isn't; this is the way of things.

There are several technologies in various forms that can recreate the information of you in a different moment or place. But that is still all part of a program, and using technology means the new time or place has had its information changed. To you, this sounds very plausible because everything is energy that can take on form or be converted to another kind of energy expression.

But what of your consciousness? Certainly, it can follow your intent to the new flux. But when is consciousness in or not in a particular flux expression? If you go elsewhere, you will still have the arkarna program attributes that you came with, including the program of the veil of forgetfulness and compartmentalisation. But you would also experience the arkarna programs of the new 'elsewhere'.

Arkarna programs are also communication and forms of 'sensing'. Some of these are associated with psychic abilities. So it shouldn't be too much of jump from your current reality to imagine that you can be in several different periods of time at the same moment. However, you presently do not understand their relationship to 'no time' and to each other.

As we communicate, try to feel comfortable with the fact that you are conversing with yourself in your many diverse projections in different mental realities. You interact with me as if I am another person in my own right, not just an arkarna. The last sentence was constructed so you did not think that you are 'self' and the rest of you is a program. You are different entities and you interact with them, enabling this information to become conscious in your dimension.

The word 'program' was used to show how you can function in other 'entity levels' at the same time. Seeing yourself as a variety of arkarna 'entities' will now be a more helpful context.

**R:** I am still struggling with the past and future being more than energetic programs. You create the impression it is an omnipresence of everything.

**HSAP:** Yes, I know – I can see that. I also know that when you express the struggle, it is your way to release the immediacy of that frustration. Life does not always have to be about immediacy or slow speed.

Let's focus on focus. There are multiple positions of focus and ways of focusing or observing. Your present awareness is predisposed to point your focus on to what you are thinking about.

Think not of points of focus but that focus exists in all

things as part of the fabric of arkarna entity programs. The focus is everywhere all of the time because it's a part of the 'all'. That's why you can move your awareness or allow it to be in any focus anywhere. Your focus is already there, but you don't have it in your mind to see it that way. Your awareness is partially hampered by concentrating upon the focus in Robert.

If I change my description from HSAP to higher self-awareness HSA I become more like an entity. However, I am also a program of awareness as you are a program of Robert awareness. I am your awareness with the abilities to see and take part in the formation of timelines.

To help you with information about who I am and how I function I will talk about the omnipresence of all things in all time.

Aqueena is not taking part in the higher self-awareness you are presently talking with. She is me, so she can be here if you think her into our presence. Aqueena is a soul embodiment expression at this level. As well as awareness and focus, she can express herself and create wonderful residual energies.

You are at a different arkarna awareness where you express and create residual energies. These things you find acceptable because you view them as energy created within the universe by you. But what you do not understand is that energy of this kind can be focus as well as awareness. You are creating within a dimension containing focus and awareness. You can bring your awareness into multiple points of focus. How does your present Robert awareness compare to our other points of awareness?

**R:** I think that would be about my perception, which keeps me to one awareness even though it pulses on and off within that dimension.

**HSA:** Prior to this book, we gave you diagrams that showed

147

how the pulses of other dimensions fitted into the non-energised part of your dimensional pulse. On that occasion, we were showing that pulse does not have to be 'one beat on and one beat off' – that faster beats of some other-dimensional realities can exist within the off mode of your pulse.

In addition to 'pulse bursts of form', awareness has to have a program that fits its bursts of awareness together into a continuous string. When you are in phase with a dimensional pulse, your awareness programs can create residual energies. If you are not in the 'on' of your earth pulse, you are in the conscious awareness of other fluxes – even though you don't remember them. The awareness there would not serve the experience of your current pulse, which is strung together on earth. The fluctuations or pulses are, of course, incredibly fast – but you are in all of them, all of the time, despite what you feel or what the earth arkarna provides for you.

If we move away from pulse to non-time, we can observe awareness as if the pulse was there or not there. This is awareness and focus existing outside of pulse. At one stage, you questioned if you could enter non-time by slowing down focus until pulse stopped. You were told that the opposite was true and, by vibrating faster, you were able to exceed its vibration. In this way, it allows you to detach focus from the pulse awareness and the ability to create energy within it.

From our current vibration, we could reinsert awareness anywhere into pulse and alter an event to change the residual energies. From our perspective, it's more like a field of energy that we can enter while not being dictated to by stimuli.

**R:** It feels so calm, but you say we are not in the 'off' of the pulse.

**HSA:** You feel as though time has stopped. Think of it this way – you and your awareness are vibrating so fast that you can now see several dimensions in the same place. It may help to imagine a sphere with lines of energy that flow around the outside and enter at the poles. A torus shape where time flows in and out of itself. Time appears as a straight line, but it bends around the surface of the sphere to disappear into itself. If the torus pulses on-off, then so will time. Gravity is as much a part of an arkarna program as is time.

All of these descriptions are metaphorical and designed to break down your current mental barriers. At present, we are only tilling the soil; we have yet to plant the seeds of ideas and see them flourish.

The occurrence of events in sequence is your experience, but it is only a program to give you that perception. So, let us take things a little more out of sequence. The shimmers could literally take you to somewhere else or give you a different sequence, like a broken glass bottle re-forming.

**R:** But that's time reversal

**HSA:** It would appear so because that's the way you look at it – through time. Let us change your perspective. Look in front and you will see large sphere different to the previous one. This time it is a mass of clouds twisting and turning as if unable to escape from a large glass ball. What's on the inside is obscured by the misty swirls across the surface. If 'thought' exists within the centre of the sphere, it will have no external or internal reference to time. Even the moving clouds are chaotic and have no sequential or rational actions.

If we now change the sphere into a torus, the clouds will disappear. A framework of energetic lines will form from the centre of the sphere. Now whatever is 'thought' at the centre affects the whole object. The torus is formed from the pulse and vibrates to the pulse. The energy that moves around in the sphere does so because it's constantly being re-formed in the pulse as part of a program. Yet, we have a fast pulsating sphere that shows lines of movement or sequential events. In this way, you can see that sequential events are also illusory because they are part of a program for movement within the pulse.

If we go back to the past, which one should it be?

**R:** Presumably, to the timelines that we walked, which shimmered between options where residual energy was created en masse or by an individual.

**HSA:** Not the other possibilities that hadn't been walked?

**R:** They wouldn't be my past they would have only been possibilities.

**HSA:** But if you went back to your past, would you know that you had?

**R:** Sorry, this is becoming a really bizarre conversation. Are you saying, if I went back with the current memory of what had been before to a point before it happened?

**HSA:** But if you didn't do that, you wouldn't be you right now – doing what you are doing.

**R:** But that's paradoxical because I can't be doing it for the first time and then do it again. That would be doing the same thing two or more different times.

**HSA:** So, as I was saying, which time?

**R:** Surely you can't have multiple times of wanting to do the same thing? The implication was that we could have multiple ways of experiencing the creative and residual energies. But that's not the same thing as this explanation of time, is it?

**HSA:** Remember time is illusory, caused by a programme of sequence. If we alter the program of sequence, you could have groundhog day. How would you make sense of non-sequential or apparently random events?

**R:** I couldn't, and it would be chaos.

**HSA:** So, we have sequential events as a program, which you see as time. In order to time travel, you come out of one sequential event and reinsert into another. You can do that as often as you like.

**R:** That's not my experience.

**HSA:** Oh really, what are you doing now?

**R:** Sequentially tapping keys while listening to you.

**HSA:** And if you make a spelling typo, you go back sequentially to alter it. If you re-read it and want to change a word to a more helpful one, you do so.

*R: I am checking typos and I wish to take issue again, but this time with the wording. At this point, what had been written the first time feels a little repetitive because it now follows the 'previous interjection'. It shows the original struggling with concepts when we have gained some of the answers to those struggles by the previous interjection. To me, it's an odd feeling of repetition – it's like crossing the same timeline or shimmer but from a different direction.*

*A: I know you are keen not to repeat information but is it actually a true repetition? You rightly surmised the feeling of passing through a small part of the same shimmer. But you are getting hung up on the fact all things should be sequential when, in fact, moving forwards and backwards is also a form of sequential movement experience. What we have all helped to write, you feel has been dramatically changed by a large information interjection. That everything we wrote and said allowed you to come to a more comprehensive awareness of 'stitching together shimmers and experiences'. That realisation should have followed at the end of the book, as it would have been in the right time order. But the truth of the fact is: unless we were helping you to re-read and check spellings, it would not have come into your awareness at all. So in that respect, it is in the right order. What we are doing right now shows how awareness can move into another focus of information within the all. It's like looking at*

151

*different versions of a breaking bottle but not in sequential order.*

*Your perception of this is going to be different from that of a reader because you know what's already been written. They are reading it for the first time, so they are not aware of your sequential experience. The interjection sits perfectly well in the flow of information to be read for the first time. This clearly shows the difference in perspectives – you will not be able to see this from the reader's perspective. Whereas I can see the energetic resonance that exists in it as information to be consumed.*

*R: Perhaps I shouldn't have interjected this time.*

*A: Well have you learnt anything from it?*

*R: Yes it could have disrupted the flow, but I would have difficulty ascertaining that because I am not coming at this as a reader. It also shakes up what is meant by a correct and meaningful sequential order.*

*A: Good, some learning then! It does, however, show that a sequence is all a matter of an awareness program. That layering information and experience requires some of the same shimmers to be re-entered.*

*R: Till it's right and then it's experienced.*

*A: No this is the point we need to reinforce. All is happening all has happened as shimmers. You can return to transmute residuals by crossing and creating on the same shimmers. However, it is more a question of trying to see the shimmers as a mental and emotional grid that interacts with itself. See it as your mental and emotional 'state' not a discordant or ancillary program but the very inner workings of who you are. It that way, you are discovering who you are while creating who you are. The actual events are not that important compared to creating and discovering you. However, that doesn't square with the paradox that in discovering yourself, you have already done so. But that's the reflection of Mowhar, and I think that's best left for another time.*

*R: Thank you, those last few sentences have helped.*

*A: Good, just pick up the typo check where you left off it will all become another aspect of the same subject – a perspective of the same shimmers on another vibration.*

*R: Straight back into questioning the comparison between typos and life.*

152

**R:** Okay, I get the analogy – but typing is not the same thing as a 'life program'.

**HSA:** Well, the text exists as a program in your computer; the information is stored in the hardware but it is also subject to pulse, which re-forms the hardware as it was in the previous pulse – or with the new word alterations. You can visit other timelines – call up other Word documents and alter those.

**R:** But that's still not my experience of my pulsating life, which appears sequential.

**HSA:** That's to do with your focus and your arkarna program.

**R:** Are you really saying that everything is random and it's only our focus programs that make sense of it?

**HSA:** Well, you accepted the shimmers in the metaphor!

**R:** Yes, you all explained that brilliantly, but that was about possibilities and the treading of my timeline.

**HSA:** It was all about possibilities but within a 'program of sequential events' or changes. However, you can also alter your experiences by changing the way you think about them. Because time is an illusion, if you do not want or need it, you can de-select the time program but retain 'sequential re-forming' within the pulse.

Try to see everything around you re-forming in bursts – become aware of the here and not here. To do this you need to vibrate exceptionally fast. We can be 'in phase' with 'pulse on' but when 'in phase' in the off moment we are not in the same realm. When your awareness returns with each pulse of your world, you are back. Your focus and awareness are in all dimensions to varying degrees. Remember, focus is part of all things, but it is awareness programs that create the experiences within them.

The mind travels when it vibrates fast enough to loosen

awareness from where you are – you can then go to another point of sequence: a before or after where you are. Time becomes excluded from sequence.

**R:** But that's not physical time travel.

**HSA:** Not in so many words. Physical time travel is also the illusion of physical movement or travel – everything is illusory, it's just a matter of what interpretation arkarna you use. Energies are re-formed in a different place all the time and, despite what we have explained repeatedly, you slip back easily into your previous thoughts about physical matter.

When you don't focus upon your pulse as a physical reality you start seeing it as a program. What was once a thing can now be viewed as an energetic format like a hologram blueprint. You can walk within it and through the blueprints of objects. Not only will you see additional things, but you will also sense them differently. It is more like melding with their essence and knowing them for what they are by their energetic resonance.

As we look before us, we can see the objects of your world pulsing on and off in holographic form. With our mind, we can spin forward through the fluctuations as if time doesn't exist. It is only our mind that perceives this movement. We can go back or forth and the hologram will change to suit the timeline we are reviewing.

From where we are now, observe it as just a program. We can again stop in any sequence, move and look around in a program of sequential events.

**R:** What you present to my mind is very clear. Thank you.

**HSA:** What part of mind energy do you think it is?

**R:** I don't know – yours?

**HSA:** Any part of the mind that vibrates to that level of arkarna program – that is us. Awareness can be in any part of 'everywhere focus', it's part of the varied programs that you can choose.

You have an earth arkarna program running which provides you with certain types of awareness and information. That arkarna is also the blueprint for how you communicate including the way to think. By unplugging part of your mind from that, you are able to be here with me and other entities. You are able to access this information because other awarenesses and entities 'of you' – are presenting this information to you in a way that sidesteps some of your arkarna constraints. Your frustration is beginning to wane. I remind you that in order for this information to arrive in your dimension, you are decoding what we present – simple bite-size pieces that make sense of some highly complex ideas.

It is so fluid here that not only can we move between different arkarnas but we can change the programs within them. We even have arkarnas that seem not to exist.

Look at the scene I am now presenting to you. There is nothing here other than an arkarna program of just the two of us as we stand together. Your mind is presenting itself to you as a 'being' when I am an 'entity arkarna of knowledge'. These levels of creator possibilities are not the same as 'experiencer levels of self', where you transmute energies through experience and deed.

**R:** That's a good explanation, thank you – so how does Orlacka, for example, change her residual energies?

**HSA:** Well, that's where you also come in, by clearing your thoughts and feelings. Some of them were created in your past lives and some of them in hers. She can direct you to certain energies, thoughts and feelings, which you can then transmute. She is able to change the ones you are dealing with because she is you.

155

**R:** I understand what you say, though I don't think I always get the fullness of what you mean. Thank you for the explanations, but these time-travel concepts do not feel complete.

**HSA:** How can we time travel if it time does not exist for us? Orlacka's energy, as well as Antemedi and Arksar, are with you.

**R:** So are you saying that I am interfacing with an arkarna program for Antemedi, Arksar and Orlacka?

**HSA:** Yes, in the main, but not always. You are getting very hung up on holding to 'what you believe you are as Robert'. You are a variety of arkarnas as well as a soul that is inter-dimensional. Arkarna is so very different from your word program. I could have used 'interface', as you did, but that seems to give it a mechanical function rather than a mental and emotional one. The more that you see yourself in the way we describe ourselves, the more like us you are.

**R:** So, to use your terminology – Orlacka is not a time traveller because she exists outside of time, but she can experience sequential movement if she wishes – she can drop one focus to have another one, which may be in any order. In that way, she can have entirely different experiences to me. I remember she said revisions to the past (me) wouldn't change who she is now unless she wants it to. So what was her past?

**HSA:** You, now, right here! And some other incarnations. You only believe that you are you because it suits you. Then you have the experiences you need. These are to face the energies created by you and your family and those of your wider 'soul group'. Incarnating is also a responsibility for several levels of soul – not that the responsibility needs to be a burden.

You are struggling because you still focus on the physical

element of your worldview. I remind you again – here, time does not exist and you can reinsert focus back into the hologram without being bound by time. Orlacka as soul can vibrate to form a different energetic shell and change an event by pinpointing mind focus on to a particular shimmer or thought that you or she has had in a sequence. In that way, it doesn't really affect who she is in her dimensions.

You are all spanning many vibrations, but it's a question of what focus experience you wish and what you create and transmute. If she wished, she could reinsert herself into a section of the hologram with dual consciousness, then it's a question of what form she wishes to take or how much energy and consciousness to put into either. You are in several consciousnesses – look at you taking notes while viewing and interacting with me.

You are just an experience of who you believe you are and what you transmute. Robert doesn't exist, he is an arkarna program of fluctuating pulse energy. After death, you are helped to let go of the idea of being who you were – that is why there was a problem accepting that earlier!

**R:** Presumably Orlacka had other lives as Arcturian in different dimensions? Has she chosen not to remember while in part focusing here as me? Am I in part her, interfacing with her arkarna program and not always her as an entity?

**HSA:** In the main, for your experiences.

**R:** So, is it a program that goes back to change her past.

**HSA:** Yes and no, it depends on what she wants to experience and what energy she wants to transmute. It's nothing to be disappointed about – the arkarna is still hers, as are you. It's the value you place on these things that gives you the difficulty you experience. It's also your belief about who and what you are that alters interpretations. Try not to see

157

yourself as Robert but that you have a focus in a holographic illusory world of pulse.

In this way, you can maintain a higher functioning awareness that's more fluid. Become more aware of the 'love interface' with the arkarna programs of yourself. At your core you are soul, but you are an arkarna because you are all these things.

Orlacka has awareness of you while in entity, not just the arkarna. You are not always aware of her direct input to you through your Robert program. Neither are you aware of the steps she sometimes takes to alter your/her experiences.

See yourself less as Robert and more as a fluid consciousness. I am happy now to pass you back to Orlacka who will talk about her direct contact with you.

**R:** Thank you.

# FIVE

Orlacka provides us with a metaphorical parable to help us understand our multidimensional lives as well as the ways we can experience them and receive enlightenment. She says the energy of the story can reside in an individual and awaken parts of the unconscious awareness.

**Orlacka:** While you are communicating through arkarna programs, I reiterate that I am very much with you. You can see me in shadow form as I stand in front of you.

There have been many times that I have assisted with different energies or thoughts – sometimes during bereavements, other times during stress or moments when you needed encouragement.

I explained that I can 'relocate' myself very easily. I am not constrained by the need to think in any particular way. However, I am here today to take you on a different path not related to recent topics. I wish to present a multi-layered fable.

## The beginning is the end

A long time ago, there was a boy who set out on a journey across a very wide desert – he was told that all would be well and he had no reason to suppose it would be any different. However, he encountered various hardships and times of great doubt. After many years, he eventually reached the other side of the desert, but as a man and all the better for enduring a few struggles.

He arrived as a much stronger and wiser person. Indeed all

was well for he was taken in by a village as their guest. He spent many hours talking to children about the things that he had learnt. However, there were many elders who were set in their ways and did not like the new ideas being told to keen and eager minds. The ideas threatened their current way of thinking and the order of things.

So, the man was banished to the desert and forbidden to speak to the children. Just out of sight, he managed to survive a reasonable distance from the village. He would help and guide other travellers in exchange for provisions. Children from the village brought him water and food so that they could listen to more of the stories and teachings.

When the town's elders heard this, they forbade the man to remain within a day and a night's walking distance of the village. However, there were two teenagers who would not be put off. And so, they occasionally made the arduous walk together when time would allow. By now the man was getting very elderly, but he continued to teach the boy and girl all that he knew. One day, when all was complete, the old man who was nearing the end of his life said, "You must make your own way in the world – wisdom has no meaning if you do not use it. Live your life and show it to others." He gave them his blessing and asked them not to return.

So the teenagers lived their lives in their different families. They used some of the knowledge, but life and family responsibilities took their toll. As they grew into a man and a woman, they did not live their life according to the wisdom they had been taught. Many years passed and everyone forgot about the old man who had long since died.

One day, the man who was once the teenager and was now a widower came across a tree in the desert when searching for a lost animal. It was exactly one day and one night's walk from the village. At once he knew it to be the place where he used to meet the old man. So he sat at the base of the tree. He relaxed in the comforting memories allowing what he had forgotten to return. A speck of energy gradually formed a portal, which gently opened to encompass the tree and him. The man could hear the voice of the old man, and when he brought his full awareness upon him he was able to see and speak with him. He travelled through the portal to a different world but he was not perturbed by the fact the old man's appearance had changed. The old man looked remarkably like he did as if he were a reflection of himself. Everything that one man did was mirrored by the other. They both sat down opposite one another and the widower realised that they both knew what the other was thinking. They did not need to speak nor say anything, there was nothing that they could give to the other that they did not have already.

After a while, a very tall, thin man approached them and asked that they should walk with him. The tall man took them to a group of 'innocent people'. They were very inquisitive and had no prejudices or fears. They wanted to know how the two men had become so compatible. It seemed to this group that there was no difference between the two men.

The taller man looked unusual because of his exceptional height, but he had nonetheless many characteristics and similarities in common with the two men. His demeanour and wisdom were so enchanting, he was quite intoxicating. He said, *"One of these men is what he is because he has been tested and he has gained what he has. The other has been taught the same things and has the wisdom of who to be. But neither one of them is valued any more or less than the other – in my eyes, they are both the same. Who did what or before the other is of no relevance when they are one and the same – who here wishes to judge them and see a difference?"*

There was no answer, but the tall man could see a boy hiding at the back of the crowd with his face tilted in shame. The crowd parted for the tall man as he walked towards the boy. The boy did not want to look at the tall man or at either of the two men. He was frightened that he would 'see a difference' and that he would be seen and judged for doing so. The two men left the side of the tall man and came forward in love. They said to the boy that he was no greater or worse than they were. They told him of Mowhar and a different way of thinking. They explained it in ways that only the boy could grasp. The boy listened intently and he became filled with new ideas and possibilities. He wanted to put these to use and have the different experiences that they would bring.

So, the tall man brought forth a camel and gave it to the inquisitive boy. It had sufficient supplies for all the years he would take to cross the desert. He told the boy all would be well because it already was. The tall man said that when he reached the other side of the desert, the boy would be a man. The boy did not fully understand, but he had no reason to suppose it would be any different because in his heart he knew he could trust the tall man. As the boy waved goodbye and started his journey, the energies changed – they shimmered and re-set themselves.

The man who was once looking for his animal began to change his awareness. He was moving back through the portal remembering who he was and that he had a family to return to. At the thought of this, he awoke at the bottom of the tree next to his lost animal with no time lost.

Upon returning to his village, the man found a commotion. It seems a traveller had just found his way there on a camel. He must have come from distant worlds because he spoke in different languages. He looked most unusual with strange eyes and glowing clothes. Because he was so different, many in the village became fearful and wanted him to go away.

The man who had returned from the portal knew in his heart who the other was. He smiled at the traveller who was once a boy, and each knew the other's thoughts as if they were their own. The villagers were still perturbed by such an odd human, so the widower took him home to his children and wider family. They made the stranger most welcome without judgement and fear. The stranger and the widower sat together as two men would. For many days they spoke with each other, but their lips did not move. They were more than a reflection of each other. They knew each other and how they thought. They knew how their hearts made them act and that filled them with love and joy.

Then, one day soon after, a shadow cast itself across the ground in coldness. This feeling made the traveller and the man stand erect in knowingness. This time they spoke aloud each other's languages as if they were their own. They knew they were needed by the villagers, despite being shunned. A crowd muttered and cowered by the edge of the one and only water well. Angst and foreboding formed deep furrows in the brows of the villagers, but it did not stop the two men from peering over the edge.

At the bottom, a reptile writhed and thrashed in the dark, spoiled water. It had defecated and was poisoning the village supply. It could not be left in there any longer so the widower lowered the unusual traveller to the bottom whereupon he spoke to the reptile.

The reptile could not instil fear in the traveller whose very body began to shine brightly with light. He put the beast upon his shoulders and climbed out of the well.

When the sun struck the reptile, it leapt from the traveller's shoulders and changed into a wicked angry man of the past. It strode about cursing and making threats. It created misery for all in its reach. Its breath was vile and black and the villagers became more afraid.

Only the man and the traveller, who could speak other languages, came forward. They tried to reason and assist the beast of a man. But the reptile man was so angry he even despised the men who were trying to help him. The creature was so filled with bile and vitriol that its own liquids began to consume him. The two men shrouded the reptile man in a cloak in order that he would not leave his stain upon the land. Though the reptile man knew he was destroying himself, he would not change – he could only hate and consume.

The two men kept the remnants of the creature in a cloak and took it to the tree in the desert whereupon a different portal opened. This time, the connection was to a faraway realm made of the same bile and vitriol as the creature. What was left of the reptile man became a part of that world and it travelled there through the portal. The cloak, however, was left behind, tarnished by the vileness. The man and the traveller laid the garment upon the ground. Light poured forth from the hearts of the men and the stains faded. The cloak transformed and became an energetic tapestry of words. It floated unseen in the ether, extolling wisdom and new thoughts. It was available in the minds of villagers if they cared to look.

The two men did not seek reward or thanks. Neither were they given nor offered. The widower's children were full-grown so he had no dependants or reasons to stay.

It is said that the man and the strange man travelled far away to discover other worlds. They have not been seen since, but then again no one can really be sure.

Some say that they talk in their minds to them.

**R:** That's unusual, not sure what to make of it.

**O:** It is different from our usual conversations. I know you are not keen on it as a fable, but there are layers of insights we can draw out. It was a way to walk you through the beginnings of some new thoughts.

The reptilian influence was discovered in its hiding place – and once it was seen for what it really was, it disguised itself as a human. To many, through millennia, it will have appeared in human form. Despite its disguise, anyone with awareness could still see its vileness. The two men were not afraid of it. The one from the faraway lands knew all about the creature because he had met such beasts before. Without fear of the creature, he was able to escort it back to its own vibrational density.

At the beginning of this story, the first man became very learned through his endeavours as he journeyed through the desert. He shared the wisdom he gained so that others did not need to undertake the same tasks. Unfortunately, not many wanted to hear his words, but a male and female progeny were primed. Listening to something new changed their thoughts and genetics. They became filled with intent, even if it did not always transpire. They had children of their own with other villagers. They were filled with more light, so it changed all who bred with their offspring – influencing all society. It did not matter they had forgotten the task the old man had set them. This was the deed that they were set to do.

When the widower came upon the land of the old hermit, he instantly remembered all he knew. The old man was able to reach from another realm and transport the man. Once there, he saw that they were the same person but with separation experiences. Their purpose was to be both a teacher and a student to each other and to learn from their different experiences. But only by separation could they learn such things. When the total realisation came, they could both accept they were each other. They would always know what the other was thinking.

Yet, there were still many other lives they could live in separation; one even as an unusual humanoid, so different he could not be understood.

This brings us to the boy who set out across the desert. Was he the boy that became the old man at the beginning of the story? Had we slipped time and returned to see the old man start his initial quest again? Or was this a shimmer and a repeating pattern of thought?

The boy was clearly someone who needed the experience of the desert. He took charge of depleting his old ways of thinking. He travelled to other worlds beyond the desert and was gone for such a long time that when he returned, he had become a different person. When he emerged from the desert, the ideas of who he was had changed so much that he became unrecognisable – except to the one person who had seen him leave as a boy. His travels and experiences in other worlds were so varied that it enabled him to remove the shimmers and repeating patterns.

The reptile man was deleted from the program of existence. Because there was no more that could be seen or done for the villagers, the student and the teacher became as one.

There are many more meanings hidden within the words above, some of which will trigger different thought processes in the readers as they relate it to other thoughts in their own inner knowing.

# SIX

Orlacka and Antemedi introduce Robert to an energetic surgeon who helps him to see in a new way by removing comforting and familiar reference points. Antemedi then takes him to a past energy where other aliens have tried unsuccessfully to engage humans in constructive dialogue. Tecca shows them their vessel and some of their technologies.

**Orlacka:** I have Antemedi with me, he wants to say a few words of encouragement.

**Antemedi:** These writings were never going to be easy. They require effort on your part but they are within your capabilities. It is what you have been trained to do. While you may not see the significance of Orlacka's story it does have correlations with many people's lives.

It was good you typed it, as shows you are open to what we have to say. The story contains energy, as do all words that are given with intent. It will reside in the subconscious as another energetic platform for anyone that takes an interest in it.

Just trust that it was given for good reason. When I said, "you have been trained", I mean that – it is the culmination of the years you have been listening to us all. Many of the ideas we are putting forward now can be expanded upon in the future.

**Robert:** Thank you.

**A:** To other matters – Orlacka and I shall remain with you so that we can hold your energy securely between us.

**O:** Look at me, what do you see?

**R:** A welcoming face though it is so very different from my own.

**O:** I could change it.

**R:** No it's fine as it is – something about getting used to how someone is.

**O:** Then you are reading the energies we are holding you in. Familiarity is what we wish to look at; it usually brings comfort or a sense that all is well. (Orlacka moves to my rear where Antemedi is.) We are walking you forwards into a new energy, you will be bound by our thoughts. However, we are also standing here to keep you steady so you do not retreat!

**R:** *(The scene)* A large humanoid looms up in front of me it then stares deep into my eyes before moving behind me to join the others. The energy pushing from behind me becomes very forceful. It moves me forward with a feeling that nothing can halt our passage, and while the movement is rather abrupt, I feel safe with all these energies around me. We come to a door and all file through except for the large person.

There is a small wooden table and stool in the middle with of a room. I know someone is here even though I can't quite see them yet.

**Person unknown (PU):** Welcome to a lesson on distraction. Communication can have elements of distraction; this is when you don't listen properly or where there is too much information. It is the familiar that distracts you from the unusual.

You are predisposed to see what you know or expect – the database has been explained. Your current way becomes familiar because you get used to expecting certain experiences.

We would like to help you dispense with as much familiarity as is comfortable. Put your head forward so that we may inspect the energetic triggers. Are you happy for me to do this?

**R:** Yes my trusted people brought you in.

**PU:** They have sought me out because of my skills with energetic surgery. You will need to stop typing for a short while.

**R:** *(The scene)* I lay face down on the lounge carpet and feel various changes taking place with minor pains. The surgeon removed what he referred to as 'dumbers'. He did this at various chakra points all the way along my body.

I became aware of several energies and thoughts being pushed to one side. For example, the removal of concepts like 'hard work, success and failure', which are forms of duality traps. I thank the energetic surgeon and he leaves, pleased to have been of help.

**A:** Good, let's see what we can bring you without the use of the familiar. No need to expect because you do not know what or even if there is anything to expect. Keep to the stillness, feel this energy – this way of being – just like the observer energy in the metaphor.

There is no time schedule, no needing to get on with typing in order that it should be finished. It doesn't require dedication or commitment nor for you to put other things aside. There is no judgement as to what is or isn't valuable. Information just is and can be part of the Isness within you. You do not need to look for new things or new ways of seeing them. If you have no filters to the words we say, then what we present will follow its course. If there are opportunities for you to grow a little within the book dictations, we will help you take them.

I do not need to explain what the surgeon did nor what it means. The drivers and dumbers are the familiar pedals and keys on the piano. There is no searching and there is nothing to search for. What comes is all part of your arkarna programs which work in conjunction with us.

Now then – please walk forwards away from Orlacka and myself.

**R:** *(The scene)* As I walk forwards my awareness splits in two – one is forward and one is back here with Antemedi and Orlacka. My forward focus comes back to me where I was but then moves to my rear about 20ft away. That awareness of me looks exactly like I do. He/me moves around me until he has increased my auric bubble. This part of my awareness returns to me and helps me feel very relaxed. I am imbued with the feeling that familiarity has no meaning or benefit.

In the distance, I see a man who walks towards me. He doesn't stop and goes straight through me and out the other side. As he does so an essence of him is left inside me – a particularly weird feeling!

Next, there are men and women coming from all directions and they also walk into me. The weird feeling cumulates; it is most peculiar – they are all in me as separate entities, but they are also the composite of me as well.

**A:** This energy will help with your periphery observation in a variety of ways. Let us move on and walk forward again.

**R:** *(Observing)* I remind myself that I should not be searching or trying to see what is here. After a short while, I feel that I have reached the edge of my understanding of what makes my world what it is. The previous programme of familiarity was also a containment field. Without it, I would have no familiar normal life boundaries, and prior to today's event, its removal would have caused great uncertainty and worry.

We continue forwards and there is a sense that we are walking over burning embers but the heat has no effect on us. We arrive at a distorted place with folded planes and sharp corners. We pass through these planes, which I can now see are energetic lines of force. We have entered a government or specialist building associated with space discovery and cutting edge science.

We are in a large square concrete room with a flat dense ceiling. The wall on the left has a window that starts at shoulder level, rising to the ceiling. It runs the full length of the wall with intermediate supports. Looking out of the high window is a man wearing a white technician's coat. He seems pleased with himself, quite ebullient and rather pompous because he has an alien in this secure monolithic room.

**A:** We cannot be seen for who we are because we are within our soul group awareness of this past event. However, you may talk with this alien being because our communication is not time dependant – the being is called Tecca.

**R:** *(Observing)* Tecca is sitting on a plywood chair with metal legs at a table in the same style. Behind Tecca on the opposite side of the room to the high-level window are a series of glass containments which span from floor to ceiling so several rooms can be seen at the same time. The man in the technician's coat has a desperation to know what Tecca is thinking.

**R:** *(I say to Antemedi)* What is this place and why am I here in what appears to be a past event?

**A:** It's okay, just flow with the energy – experience this as if you were the soul that was here when this happened. Though it will be an alteration in part because of your involvement.

**R:** Should I talk telepathically with Tecca?

**A:** I have introduced myself – he can see that you are here in another vibration.

**R:** Hello, Tecca. I hope they are treating you well.

**Tecca (T):** As well as you would expect in a place like this. Several of us arrived here of our own free will. I remained, wishing to speak to a human earth consciousness that would understand what I was saying. I can communicate with these people including the person you see. But they really can't understand why I say the things that I do – they don't have the conceptual ability and flexibility of mind to understand me.

Of course, the dialogue is all about what they want. We are a race unknown to them and they wonder how we are compatible with their atmosphere. My vibrational existence here does not rely upon what they think. They are obviously very cautious about contamination, so this building is about containment as well as incarceration. They are unable to accept that germ growth is vibrational and dependent on the body's acceptance of that vibration.

Let me show you these two energies, which look like white rods. These energies cannot be seen or detected by the humans. They can be placed in opposing corners of this room when it is time for me to leave. The rods will disrupt time within the space between them. At the moment they appear in slow motion before activation. When I activate them I will be relocated. The humans will have no idea that this is possible nor realise we can alter timeline programs so that memory becomes inaccessible.

We will be leaving no trace of our visit and the humans will not remember us; our friends the Andromedans are well aware of our presence. Perhaps another time we may meet different humans and our presence will be more welcomed.

172

Thank you for bringing your consciousness here. I can see your thought processing is interesting – it makes me realise that beyond the time you are experiencing, there are future possibilities for better communication. When I return would you like to come with me?

**R:** Yes, but this moment I am not entirely sure what this meeting has been about and why I've been taken back to this time.

**A:** Well, there has been much consternation about the proliferation of nuclear weapons. At different times many beings have tried to help humanity to see the futility of these devices. As Tecca says, humans only want to hear what is beneficial to nations' and individuals' self-interests.

We may now go with him. We are not fully resonant here and as unseen we can help place these resonators around the room. Tecca did this by himself before. He mentally projected the rod energies to those opposing positions. He did it in a different dimension to the concrete buildings. The rods were energised then he was relocated.

**R:** This really is sci-fi stuff.

**A:** Not really, it depends on which dimensional reality you are interacting with.

**R:** There is no corroborating evidence to show any of this is real – does it even have a place in the communication book that you are presenting?

**A:** Let us go with Tecca and see what he says.

**R:** *(The scene)* As the rods do their work there is a soft vibration of white light. When it settles, we find ourselves in a craft of some kind. It has unusual curved sweeping edges and ceilings with different variations of grey and cream. There's plenty of light but I can't see any lighting units – the light just seems to exist by itself. Obviously, I'm only there in a part of my consciousness and continue to type on the keyboard. I feel a bit 'wobbly' in the consciousness in their dimension, so they sit me down to help regulate my energies. Tecca is quite a bit smaller than us and his presentation is more 'light' than anything else.

**A:** Reformatting – It's similar to what Orlacka talked about before – specific focus and energising vibrational patterns.

**R:** With or without technology?

**A:** Technology can enhance certain vibrational patterns. It is part of the reason for you to be shown the events today – listen to what he has to say.

**T:** Now that my energy is vibrating as a more complete focus and not tuned into that lower dimension, you can see my fullness. I understand you have been having conversations about time, the greater abilities of mind and how the mind can work in conjunction with technology. I know you have been told about technology and the self-aware programs. Indeed, self-aware programs are part of the function of technology and vice versa. Protocols exist as part of that but they can be overridden.

Anyway I shall put that aside for the moment. I wish to say "welcome", it gives us joy to have a human consciousness on board with us – I have brushed up on my teaching skills.

**R:** Because we moved from a previous timeline, what time frame are we in now or what sequential event?
*(Agghhh! got a high pitch noise in my ears!!! – Quite painful.)*

**T:** There – that was helpful; you should be able to hear me better now. We are not in time. You are stuck trying to locate 'where and when', and that holds you back to those parameters.

174

**R:** So was any of this real? Though I guess that's to do with comprehension of different mental realities.

**T:** I know you have had conversations like this one already. We have similar technology to the Andromedans, which allows us 'information access' which will be pertinent to what we wish to know. We can accesses this mentally or through technology reinforced programs that run alongside our own arkarnas. I am happy to use the word arkarna for I am aware of your limitations even in your totality.

I am not within your particular soul relationship but I am still able to download or attach myself to the 'knowing of you'. It is all part of arkarna at this level. It flows in the moment like the shimmers you have seen. Things adjust to suit the circumstances. The 'knowing' works according to the different dimensions and to the particular parameters of the species using them.

I know all this sounds fantastical – that's understandable. While you were given help to let go of some familiarities, 'dimensionality' isn't an easy thing to see in completeness from your level. I am, however, happy to try some different explanations. I have been briefed about you while in another arkarna program, which was all a part of the rationale for this meeting. Our realms of consciousness have very different rules that govern them. Come follow me to where it's a little less busy.

**R:** *(The scene)* There's a lot of activity with various members of crew or passengers with tasks. They are fully aware of our focus and vibration so give us the appropriate space. Antemedi and I lower our heads, as the doors and openings are designed for smaller occupants. The ceiling in the first room seemed to stretch up and up, perhaps part of an optical illusion caused by the light 'just existing'.

We are now in an elongated room with a much lower ceiling. At various points there are holographic screens floating above a long table.

They initially appear flat but the energetic aspect of the screens moulds its projections to suit the operator's needs. At one, a female has extended both her hands and forearms into the hologram. From the side view, it is a 'sketchy energetic image' and her hands are moving about in wispy energies. She is engrossed with what appears to be a planting scheme.

As I pass behind her the hologram has a more intense energetic projection. It becomes 'formative' just like a 3d reality and I feel I could actually walk into it. The colours are so vivid and it's so real that she must actually have her hands in another reality. Perhaps the energy of the screen wraps around like gloves into another world.

She turns and smiles at me, hearing my thoughts. She is very petite with dark hair and very wrinkly skin. She seems to be a different race to Tecca. She refocuses and by thought is able to roll forward the image within the screen. This means she moves much further into where she is working while still being seated. She is moving around in another reality while she is still here.

**T:** Seeing something is better than a description. This lady is not one of our usual crew, she is here to help with a replanting scheme for an ancient walkway. It was designed to radiate different energetic resonances. Each plant has different tones and sounds so as you pass them you can detect the various vibrations. It is a way of making a musical or harmonic walk. I hasten to add it is not your earth world.

**R:** As we move along, the ceiling gets lower still. Tecca moves to the other side of a table and I sit opposite him with Antemedi on my left.

I am aware of Orlacka's energy on my right, but it is faint.

**T:** Welcome properly.

**R:** He shows us a diagram of the vessel. It has an elliptical shape and that's why the spaces near the edges get smaller. It has several levels and compartments but this is the functional floor. He explains the edges radiate a specific energy, which encapsulates everything. It's a large enough vessel but apparently, it can alter in shape!

**T:** I know you don't yet understand dimensionality fluctuations. Space is non-local. That means it's the same everywhere but perceived differently because of the flux or pulse of different dimensions. If you perceive a single point, then that single point is everywhere and it is everything. However, there are even levels beyond that form of oneness.

At the moment this vessel is vibrating to a dimensional level of oneness. We are everywhere and nowhere because there is no location relative to other things around us. However, we are slightly distorting the Isness because we have created a point of space within it. Actually, the whole of our ship is many points in the Isness because of its fluctuation in pulse. It is a dimension within another dimension – not in its usual or casual dimension.

Outside the ship 'the everywhere and nowhere' is all the same before it gets different at deeper levels within the Isness. It's a bit like a mirror of a mirror in all directions. But let's keep it to these levels of non-locality. As I said, we are residing in a different dimension within that. We are not travelling anywhere because there is nowhere here and nowhere to go, but at the same time it's an interconnection to everything that you can't see – so in a way it's everything. If we wish to materialise we change the vibration and the shape of the craft to suit the dimension. You could see it as an energetic suit, which we can phase up or down.

It is unusual and you don't understand all I am saying. If I lift up my arm, I extend the energy of the ship because it moves with my arm. I said a short while ago that it could change shape if it needs to because it is interactive with us. Changing shape can be for several reasons, but what I have shown is intent. The awareness programs of our vessel interact with us. We would not normally do this and I only did so to show you what is possible.

**R:** So your vessel isn't solid.

**T:** Come on Robert! I thought you were past that – everything that's solid is a programme of energy. It depends at what level of programs you are working at, which in turn corresponds to the relevant vibrating energy and information.

**R:** I can't get my head round that.

**T:** You are here with me and you believe your solid part is on earth typing as we experience these things. That's because you have become used to the phrase 'pliable mind'. That keeps you to bending and moving what you know or believe. Of course, that is true for what you currently know in terms of the ownership of self.

In this instance, it's more useful to see the mind as a variable fluxing energy. When talking with us or viewing things at distance, you are there by virtue of being connected to all space through non-space. A place and a concept that is everywhere at the same time. To help, you could imagine it as similar to the 'nothing' before the formation of Mowhar and the creation of perpetual pulses.

**R:** Okay, at one level we are 'everything' but we can be in different focus points by virtue of the fact we have non-space within us and outside of us. No distance can be measured because there is nothing to measure it with and there is no space. I still find it difficult to comprehend and conceive.

Should I accept that like nothingness there is no way to conceive of it because it doesn't exist, otherwise it would be something? But paradoxically it must exist as 'non-existence'. Why am I seeing the outside of the craft as a creamy beige colour?

**T:** What is non-space meant to look like if it exists as non-existence?

**R:** So is this to do with the rates of pulse?

**T:** A place of no pulse and non-creation – the place before Mowhar.

**R:** From nothing is everything.

**T:** And vice versa, it is paradoxical.

**R:** If you can be anywhere, why is the vessel still in nowhere? How do you locate a place you want to go to when you have no reference point in non-space?

**T:** Good question, but you have been shown that concept before when you reach for a place and the rest of you follows the reaching. It is clear to see that your memory access is not like ours. However, to widen that answer I would say it also depends on the dimension you wish to create in non-space and what one you wish to exist at.

**R:** Interesting – that wasn't on my radar.

**T:** With previous explorations, you have entered finer dimensions by vibrating faster. You have felt this to be going inwards as if entering your centre; a bit like heading towards a small door at the end of a tiny corridor. Things get smaller and smaller, but when your mind passes through the door everything gets incredibly big.

Bigger than the dimension you came from because having gone through to your centre, you find that all centres are connected to all centres everywhere – infinite. That is your perception about vibrating in another dimension when you are in the same vibration as it.

**R:** You know a huge amount about what I've been thinking. I find it extraordinary you know me so well.

**T:** Programs within programs and accessible arkarna programs working in conjunction with mine. I know you find that hard, but it is none the less true. I know everything about you to the smallest detail as well as knowing nothing about you. The information forms as I need it because the arkarna programs at these levels allow us to interact with one another – as if we are the other having full knowledge of them. Like the Andromedans and Arcturians, we can use technology to enhance programs.

Initially, your mind has conceived that we are in a craft that creates a bubble within non-space. An alternative, more helpful way to see that is creating a bubble of no space around us but that it has no outer edge. One shows 'infinite and nothingness contained' in a bubble whereas the other is 'nothingness with no desire to see if it has a boundary'. The latter best suits the situation because of the way your mind 'seeks things' and of course, seeking in nothingness is futile. We are in a bubble of a bubble with no edge.

**R:** But if you are in non-space you must have flux or pulse to exist.

**T:** Yes. I will help you with your feelings because if you feel 'you understand' you won't be feeling that 'you don't understand'. I do however need to expand upon 'the reaching' for the benefit of the reader.

Now then – let's say you look out of a window and see a star that you would like to travel to. Feel that you are reaching your arm all the way across space because your arm also exists in non-space and non-space exists with it. When you have your fingers on the tiniest spec of space dust next to the star you want to go to – you have created a link through non-space.

You have your connection you can see it – all you then do is pull on the dust particle and allow the rest of your body to enter non-space and catch up to where your finger is. A bit like turning yourself inside out or pulling a jumper off your head.

**R:** That had slipped my mind. The metaphor is the same one Antemedi used when explaining the process to me. It really helped me to 'feel I could understand' even though the technological process behind it would be incomprehensible to me.

**T:** Yes, it is a good metaphor and yes, you do have a poor memory. If you were like me and had a better 'access interface to knowledge' then your memory would be no problem, it wouldn't be needed for that way of thinking. How do you think you would cope with accessing all current knowledge that's been shared by humanoids?

**R:** There would be differences between accessing what I knew and had forgotten and what I wasn't aware of. Any new information that was way beyond my boundaries would be difficult to comprehend unless there was context. I would need the right arkarna programs in place to deal with accessing information like that. I take your point 'just accessing' is a very different way of thinking and certainly falls within the theme of this book.

**T:** There are levels of you that undertake these tasks I have described. There are many, including Orlacka next to you, whose consciousness is not at full volume.

**R:** Tecca, this has been great, it's helped a lot. But I still struggle with the 'not being me'. It's not easy to accept that Robert is an experience. I realise I am looking to see which part of me I am and I haven't fully entered a focus to see that I am all those aspects of me.

**T:** You can't think your way out of a feeling. Maybe you should work on changing your feelings. You have been told about the timeline shimmers and entering a program that forgets. These are vibrations where you have no need to remember. Becoming more fully conscious is very comfortable when you let go of yourself. It is a feeling that you are coming home and remembering what home was.

Remembering that you are other beings, a series of beings or lifetimes past and future. It may take a little adjustment to a new series of memories, but it will be pleasant. It will be the same as you do every morning. Initially, you wake and think, "Where am I? – oh yes, I'm in my bedroom and I am me".

**R:** Getting in touch with that feeling of being home in myself is making me a bit emotional. Thank you for all your efforts. I still have lots of questions such as – why did we meet in the particular circumstances we did?

**T:** Because I wished to interact with and experience the consciousness of evolving human energy. I am glad to have assisted, and there will be more I can help with. Orlacka will be here very shortly, her energy is becoming more focused.

**R:** Tecca, did you infer previously or did I mishear that there was another element to non-space – a sort of reverse side?

**T:** Indeed I did. Orlacka and I will outline that if you like.

**R:** Can you tell me more about you?

**T:** I am not keen on definitions 'being this or that'– it is a focus of comparison. You will put me in a box when in reality I am multidimensional and can move easily within different projections – I have many lives. That is not what you wanted to hear but it is far better to place no values on the difference between us. The information I supply is more beneficial than trying to be specific in describing what is difficult to describe. In any event, you would not understand some of the descriptions of us nor our ability to interface in different forms. These levels are exceptionally fluid, and a simple definition will not suffice.

As more unfolds in these sessions, you will understand and the descriptions will feel more specific because they need to be all-encompassing. Specific to a point but all-encompassing, and so Mowhar shows herself again. Of these things and more of me, you will learn in the months ahead.

**O:** That is so, there will be more revelations. Tecca and I could be considered as good friends. We are not of the same race, and our understandings are complementary but not necessarily the same. When we meet, we can see possible alterations that are worth implementing in our arkarna programs. This mainly involves inter-race communication.

You have been given some concepts of non-space. All possibility and no possibility with no distance or separation. However, you feel this space is a general emptiness and you have an ambivalence to it as if it has no worth.

**R:** Well surmised.

**O:** It's not entirely like that. When we talk of higher vibrations or faster-vibrating energies you try to locate them in their relationship to one another. Higher isn't up and lower isn't down; they are all intermingled within the same space.

The sea has salt in it and is also made of oxygen and hydrogen but on the face of it, it's a liquid. We could say that water is a dimension and that aquatics are intermingled within it. There are places where the water dimension doesn't exist, where instead there is land and air. All of this is within pulse 'here and not here', all a vibration.

There are other vibrational dimensionalities that can exist in the same places, but they do not have to. Humans have connectivity with other dimensions through their multidimensional self. This means several dimensions exist within your aura. These are external to your physical body (within the air) and internal within the flesh, bones, nervous systems and DNA. The multidimensional nature of things does not need to occupy the same places.

A place is a specific location, whereas space is bounded even if it is a void. Some dimensions don't exist everywhere, but even though there may be pockets or voids, they are still all connected by non-space. It is as if there is no space between them – that they are one and the same and there is no division. In addition to connection by soul multidimensionality, there are portals and other connections. Some portals connect to similar vibrating densities others connect to different vibrations. It is possible to see some of these as energetic threads. Like the silver cord from your mother's dying body to where she stood removed from the body pain.

Different cords exist within thoughts, particularly when thinking about other people or by linking to them. Another example would be concerts or places of joyous meetings. The cords from the people might appear to be complex but at the same time quite beautiful as certain emotions are shared and released. Joint meditations and spiritual singing also produce cords. This is inter-dimensional energy, which moves through non-space.

We explained that filters were once placed around the earth to contain its negativity. These filters also inhibited the connecting cords and portals as well.

184

The more we describe the 'way of energy' the easier it will be to accept you are beings of light utilising a body shell in a pulse. In a comparable way, higher dimensional beings have 'light projections' as bodies. As you accept this you will begin to see that your physical body is a manifestation of your vibrational resonance – what you think, believe and feel you are. You are light beings every one of you.

Perception is another matter. Some vibrations are close to one another and can appear as a combined unit. Metaphorically, for example, space encompasses the sun, moons, planets, water, air and land because they are all part of that dimensional pulse. Yet, there are other dimensions of the earth that are not seen because they are vibrating differently.

Of finer vibrations within a vibration, we have already mentioned that earth will upgrade to a fifth-density resonance. You have heard how this will impact upon the mental and emotional self as well as the arkarna body programs for your physical projections. This means that there will be no pockets left of what was before.

After progressing through fourth, the fifth-density energies will be omnipresent, just as third-density once was. Anything that remains of before will not be 'seen' as a pocket within – all will be connected through non-space and it won't be seen for the reasons I explained above. However, there will be historical points of the earth where portal connections existed to other densities both higher and lower.

The later ones will fade or be closed up by specialised energy workers. The energetic chords between you all, I likened to mini portals of connection in non-space. In the future, there will be no pockets to go through by way of non-space. That which becomes fifth-density will become all.

**T:** Not only can planets upgrade to finer vibrational densities but so can other higher density realities. It has been a commonly held thought that all densities exist within exactly the same places. That is not so – dimensional light beings have within their aura 'portals and connections' to their other-dimensional self-projections, which can be in a different place and space. What is consistent is non-space inside and outside the self, it is everywhere and nowhere.

There are places on earth and other planets where ethereal and subterranean beings exist in alternative vibrations. Being below in the bedrock and stone has no effect upon them. It just doesn't exist; it is a completely different realm.

Others can use minds to alter information fields to create or change that which is around them – including their own projection and form. I am not referring to the regressives, who live in underground tunnels or those that vibrate just beyond third-density. Any that try to remain will be in their own dimensional pockets and not part of fifth-density. Their dimensional vibration pockets can be taken through non-space to places where like is of like (by the work of other benevolent beings).

So you may wonder what is this non-space we have been trying to describe and is there anything beyond that?

I could start by saying it's a reversal of what is currently known – an upside-down or back-to-front. If I said it was another universe, then how many non-spaces are there and are they interconnected? Do they occupy spaces in the same way we have just described or do they have other parameters?

I am giving you questions to which I have the answers – the questions are 'possibilities and free'; as soon as you try to disseminate and understand them you start to restrict possibility which is the possibility of me to answer in a fuller way.

Is it the other side the 'off-pulse'? The other valve of a beating heart? How many connections are there to alternative realms on the other side of your own? The word Mowhar seems to have similarities in the *here and not here* of the pulse and the *nowhere and everywhere* of non-space. Paradox seems to contain creative and destructive energies because that's your take on things good or bad. You might come to the idea of *creative or not-creative energy*. But try to see it as *energy pulse* and *no energy* – that it is perpetual and self-perpetuating. New matter can form in parts of the universe but that is the transformation of energies within pulse.

The creation of pulse no longer exists. The dimensional pulses have a degree of similarity to Mowhar and paradox. The energy of the on-pulse is neutral and can be used or transformed according to needs and arkarna programs. The creations are the degrees of blending between positive and negative energies when are then made live by the pulse. You can see that positive and negative division exists in everything on earth as it struggles to evolve. It is often said you could not find your way in the light unless there were shadows to show you the way.

Souls move against entropy towards the light that exists on one side of non-space. The word entropy, unfortunately, signifies chaos and disorder, which is in part true, but the arkarnas are order and meaning so entropy does not need to exist when you no longer need it.

On the other side of non-space, there is darkness, which can only exist by feeding from light or upon itself. It is the antithesis of the other side. Some refer to these as 'dark dimensions', but that infers they exist on one side of non-space. It's more a question of how the portals through non-space affect the other side.

This negative had to form, it was a part of Mowhar and thus, you might think, ultimately a part of us. We know one could not exist without the other. It seems to be a good choice to be a creator rather than a consumer of light. But good or bad doesn't come into it. It's about the choice of what to give or accept as you move through aspects of paradox. It's about what you wish to experience – to create and nourish or not. Within a 'blending of paradoxical expressions', some beings have extinguished much of their light but have been known to reverse their demise. Others, like the example of the reptile man, decide otherwise.

The dimensions where significant blending occurs are places of major conflict between dark and light.

As a light being, I have no fears in the way that you do. I know what my mind and heart are capable of and darkness could not take a droplet of energy from me. Some regressives within and on the edge of the blended areas are able to feed upon fear energy and emotional negativity. They create fear in others because it sustains them.

The energy of personal actions/creations leaves resultant energies, which inform your arkarna programs. So if resultants can be removed and different programs put in place, then future negative creations are less likely to form. Some of the negative energy created has been consumed by regressive entities that regurgitate it as their resultant energy-containing corrupted programming. They link and feedback to humanity to create more of the same.

A good way to look at this would be to use a metaphor of an inflated party balloon tied off at the mouthpiece. The middle of the knot would be non-space as there is no space for the air to escape. The small wrinkly section one side of the knot you would have blown through, would be the negative energy potential on the other side of non-space knot. The balloon cannot be popped and has 'space' to grow and change within. The wrinkly side is open-ended and cannot be filled with light nor can it contain anything. 'Regressive' simply means to devolve – the opposite of evolve. When there is no light and no energy converted from neutral into fear, there is nothing to sustain the darkness. The only thing that can be consumed is others similar to itself. Gradually, like the end of an umbilical cord, the knot will shrivel and fade. Your need to feed and link to such places will fade.

Each of you can link to what you wish; it's not just the arkarna of mankind. You can create your own portals by intent. Of course, if one wants to go retrograde, that's still possible but that will be by choice and not external influence and manipulation in the future. Your free will cannot be interfered with, though many a light being would come to show where choices lead you. Other doorways and portals that exist to higher dimensions will be easier to access as each of them becomes filled with more and more light. When fear and distortion are no longer part of your arkarna, you will need a different metaphor to the balloon in order that you may encompass that new way of being.

**R:** A very good metaphorical representation. What of other dimensions and portals?

**T:** As I said, energy can be transformed to generate new possibilities. While the balloon was part of an explanation, you need to remember that there are pockets. Points with connections to both sides of non-space and some portals are connected with some very unhelpful humans that seek to align themselves with what they think is a power for their own use. Let me dispel fears that these darker realms can have their way. There is no need to put thought energy into 'fear that this is not to be' – Just follow the heart.

Our use of non-space is different from the above metaphorical description because it has no connections to lower dimensions and is completely neutral for us. That's why I said it would need a revised metaphor to encompass the removal of 'fear and no fear' from your dimensional arkarna programs.

In addition to creating pockets for craft, we can also create mini-worlds with no other exit portals than the ones we intend. These could be viewed as managed containment pockets with only an exit to 'like' vibrations. This is similar to the portal for the remainder energy of the reptile man. We also talked about pockets in fifth-density during the transition.

**R:** Could the regressives get through those portals or pockets that have lower density exits?

**T:** It's an impossibility. We utilise altered arkarna programs. Our speed is so fast it doesn't exist in the slow rates of such darkness and in any event, we are not in their space.

The subject of negativity did need a sufficiently wide explanation. That's because it is relative to *ways* of thinking. We thought it could be understood more easily by placing it against the backdrop of non-space. Let it be as I have said. You may now move to other matters of stimulation.

**O:** Thank you Tecca it was good for Robert to hear this from a different source. Using different visuals you showed other-dimensional communications, non-space, connections through portals and vibrational pockets (*At this point Tecca fades away*)

**R:** Can you give more insightful descriptions of Tecca?

**O:** These are beings of resonance and they stretch much further over time and beyond it than I do; they can be seen in lots of different ways and lots of incarnate forms. But what is incarnate? For them, it is only a projection, and they have no concern as to how you may see them. They are seen as blue wafts of energies – sometimes as feathers or wings.

They are known by different names for different appearances. At times you may see beyond and through them to the cream/gold energy beyond. That is why they are not often seen because they resonate beyond any concept of self. If you were primarily viewing them at one of their higher projections through your ideas of self they would simply 'not exist for you'. But, as Tecca said, he will give more expansive explanations in the months ahead.

**R:** In the previous dialogues other Mowhars and other universes were mentioned.

**O:** Well that moves quite a way from 'consciousness and alien communication' so I would like to move back to a previous theme already covered – life after death.

**R:** I thought that was comprehensively covered; it encompassed how choices of next life were part of many levels of communication.

**O:** It may have been sufficient for you but not necessarily so for all others. Because you have seen and spoken with deceased individuals, you accept this as a matter of fact. Most people don't experience life and communication in quite the same way you do.

So, I am going to be quite factual. There is no need to reassure or give someone continual assurance. One begets the need for the other. On death, no one will go to the non-space portal but instead to internal ones that lead to the light. Between incarnated lives, there still exists levels within levels but the veil program of forgetfulness does not hamper these. These levels are attached to the vibratory nature of inner-self and higher guidance. While there is time for reflection, there is also relaxation, joy and learning. There are no pressures and love abounds. Other vibratory levels exist within this over-arching arkarna where like energy will be drawn to like. Thus some areas have less light than others, though it is all the same reflective plane. It is not a place to live eternally, it is a place

191

of transition towards the source or the altering of what you were into a program of what you want to be.

Not everyone returns to earth, but some souls on the transitional plane are already eager to revisit it when it becomes fifth-density. More people are interacting with guides who are showing alien humanoid connections. As more of them are born on earth, they will raise awareness of our souls' wide and varied connections.

The guidance is given within loving arkarna programs, but individuals end up choosing by their own free will. They cannot move to a vibration that they are not willing to become compatible with. On the transition realm, it is also possible to explore further afield. It's easier to become aware of 'exceeding the self' and interacting with higher density beings and realms.

Souls can also let go of the reincarnation loop within the parameters outlined above. Tecca explained how the loss of self could be a gentle awakening.

**R:** You haven't really said much more than you did previously.

**O:** Well I was recapping in order to provide slightly different overlays. For those that ascend to their hearts they may as they wish. But their hearts may then desire to express in different ways. There are multiple choices but 'love of self' is so much a part of arkarna that the self may become totally at one with love.

Some will transcend to higher vibrational densities where their consciousness already exists in freeform (as we have shown with other beings living in higher arkarnas). The 'morning awakening' was a gentle way to describe this, but in order for this to happen there has to be a purging and a complete letting go of self before the process starts. It also requires the actual ideas and concepts of self to become dysfunctional and redundant. You will need to transmute every part of who you are by your own choice. It could be seen as a process of assimilation, but those words convey insignificance of self instead of magnificence.

Like you we will not live forever, we will transmute again – very few wish to continue as the same expression. Yes, our lives may be counted in thousands of years compared to your own, but sooner or later we feel that we have done what we need to. Sometimes that can be the re-unification of our lower split consciousness returning to us. Unification energy transfers work both ways during your earth experience enlightenment. Don't get hung up on who you are or when you are.

**R:** Just as you said that my memories of Cytith and Andromedan lives came to me, but there is no sense of sequence one before another.

**O:** In a way, that depends upon your ability to accept several points of focus without the desire to remain a particular version.

**R:** Well the Robert version will disappear.

**O:** Undoubtedly, as will the Orlacka version and all of those that you have talked to in their projections. Arksar showed you several very different dimensional expressions of himself which you sketched.

**R:** And you are hermaphrodite, but Aqueena isn't?

**O:** You want a definition that fits the parameters of what you have learnt to date. Because you don't see it any other way doesn't mean you can put the wrong peg in the wrong hole.

Let us now enter a space with gentleness and the minimum of description. The sublime is full of knowing as if it already exists for you.

**R:** So at some level, I've already done this?

**O:** Gentleness is the key – let my words flow slowly with purpose and without disturbance. Whatever exists in my communication does – let it not be questioned, referenced or distorted. I have no need to challenge you at this particular moment. My thoughts for you are not conditional upon any outcome unless it is bound in love of thyself by the whole self.

There comes a time when all transmute to something else – to another aspect of themselves. When you see someone dying in peacefulness, often they have already let go of anything that mattered to them – they have little attachment to your world.

They know in all their knowingness that all is well and that they are ready for transition. They are wrapped in love and nothing has significance to the peaceful simplicity of being at one. Much of what you still question, talk about and view is far from the oneness I have described. You are still so much you – so much so that you cannot feel and know what else you are.

We have taken you on journeys to release you from concepts of belonging – through the land of mirrors, which show only you until you see you are nothing. We show you what exists beyond yourself. It doesn't mean that you do not exist but that you hold to no description of who you are. You know that in any moment you are able to experience what comes without the desire to have it or not have it.

All experience can be welcomed and the experience does not need to define you. Fear does not exist in that state nor does doubt or desire. You felt this as blandness, but I can assure you it is no such thing. The mind and heart are free because they are not constrained by your levels of arkarna.

Beyond your reflection, you can see your past creations, born of the need to express in order that you become someone or something. Once you realise these were the old ways, they can

*Journey Through the Land of Mirrors, a painting
by Robert Lomax*

only but abate and fade. The further from these realms you move, the closer you become to others. They become extensions of you as if you are an extension of them. There is no division – you are they and there is nothing between you. There is nothing that needs to be put in place or done.

What we have then in common is the desire to change the programs of the past, which are the programs of the future at the same time. It's all laid out in its grandness – the future and the past and what we can be. Variation does not occur from any value of the past because we have removed that energy from those programs. Even though such programs could exist, they have no light and no purpose.

If this were not so, the *future you* would be a definition based upon the parameters of self and the need to be. The *future you* no longer has the need to exist and he doesn't come into existence because you put no light in him. In this way, the past and the future become irrelevant for us – for me. Who I am is not so much irrelevant as 'not relevant'; only by clearing the past and the energy of the past could we ever exceed time and its limitations. The future and the past become constructs. They constrain us to specific parameters and here we have none – except paradoxically 'the parameter is that we have no parameters'.

**R:** So your purpose is to evolve – to unify?

**O:** I have 'no purpose' as well 'as purpose' but neither of these can define me. I don't make decisions in the way that you do. I am decision and I am not. As soon as you hold to one you have the other. Duality has no foothold in me, none whatsoever.

**R:** I always thought that singularity would be the answer or the release from duality.

**O:** Not in the way that you see it as an answer. I repeat there is no *future me*. I do not evolve. I may change the parameters of my arkarna programs. I may transmute my energy to another dimensional reality. But I do not evolve – what should I evolve to? Certainly, nothing constrained by time. It is evolution that has its feet in time. If I am to evolve more, it means I am not evolved enough now – that definition says I am not enough. I am evolved to the point of not seeing that I am evolved or not. It has no significance in these levels of love.

**R:** You have exceeded every concept I once held of you. I am glad you have taken the 'time', if I can use that word, to keep repeating these things until I was more able to grasp the chasms between our worlds. Every time I think something is ground-breaking something else dumbfounds me – Incredible concepts and arkarna programs beyond humanity's concepts.

**O:** I have all the time in the world because it is not relative to evolution or progress.

**R:** If I am still evolving does it mean that at some level you are held back because we are of each other?

**O:** If I am evolved there is no more to evolve into – there is no more to be and no infinity but that cannot be so because paradoxically there is no limit. Evolution is a word that has no context here – evolution is still a value by virtue that it is comparison with its feet stuck in time.

As for our connectedness, that has no bearing on me. If I am not bound by time while you are – it has no comparable effect to be made by stating it.

**R:** All my words and thoughts unravel in your presence. I am not offended, perhaps surprised, that such things can exist like this. All that you have challenged has enriched my life.

**O:** Now that you listen in gentleness and love, perhaps so. No need to determine thoughts and questions – what is presented is 'what is'.

At last, you hear me as I wish you to hear me – more as I know myself. In doing so you will be more able to meet the next beings I wish to introduce.

**R:** It is just so peaceful, everything seems to be in the right place or that there is no wrong place. *(Coming towards us are three very tall lanky beings that are only just perceivable in the light that surrounds them.)*

**O:** These are twelfth-dimensional souls. I will use your

language even though it is not appropriate. I could say these are very ancient beings but they have existed outside of time in their realms for so long that they no longer need concepts of what you may consider as being life. It is as if what you are does not compute.

You have assumed that all higher beings understand lower dimensions. It is not that they don't or can't understand because they have no knowledge. It is that they do not choose to have it in their consciousness mainframe anymore because it serves them no purpose. For me, understanding serves a purpose even though I am not bound by time or your reality.

You might think of them as angelic but angel form does not create residual energy by expression. Angels are extensions of your soul in purity – they have unconditional love and understanding for humanity. But that is another matter from the one I wish to present.

I will be interceding between you both and buffering some of your excesses. I would like you to be as calm and accepting as you can be. Initially refrain from asking questions or even trying to process what you are hearing. They would not welcome some of the darker thoughts you have. Even though you are kind of heart and bear them no malice you appear to them as a dark shadow. See I am showing you how you appear to them.

**R:** Ooh! That's grim I look distant and empty and full of discord.

**O:** At times I will show you what they see and feel. This will help you to understand more about them by allowing some of your energy to mix with them through me. It is in part my energy but as we share a commonality of self, there shall be no disparity or confusion.

**R:** *(They welcome us both but look to Orlacka to communicate.)*

198

**O:** They ask what you hope to gain from this meeting?

**R:** A little more understanding of their realm and whether we have any relationship to it. But I am happy to let go of my questions and be open because I do not know what is possible to be gained by either of us. *(I can see them nodding. Orlacka tells me that we are to follow them into a greater resonance that will enhance our communication. After a while, I can see a room with a window looking out on to the universe. They have green lumpy skin and large purple eyes. They have long arms and insect heads – a mantis/humanoid meld. Mantoid* **(M)** *speaks via Orlacka.)*

**M:** He has accepted our appearance, which means he can accept our wisdom and understanding. Welcome traveller, we think Orlacka has been a little too cautious about our sensibilities; we are more robust than she made out. However, we can see the gentility and calming was more for your willingness and the ability to trust her so that you were not startled by our appearance.

We see the reasons why – and yet she is correct – what you hear as a direct communication from us is in part through her. Not so much a third party transfer as a mutual connection between us all. There is so much you do not know and so much possibility that exists across the universe. Your mind could not conceive or hold as a possibility such varieties of expressions and form. Much of this form expresses itself in dimensions much finer than your own vibration.

**R:** (One of them opens up a bony hand with long fingers and shows me a bright sparkling orb, which creates 'visions'. Within it, I can see vegetation and two of the mantoids walking side by side inspecting flowers and plants. It reminds me of the harmonic plant walking areas I saw being reconstructed earlier.)

**M:** Everything you are being shown has a degree of inter-connectedness; you did not come here by chance. We and other beings are able to interact on levels that affect different dimensions of realities in the same space. That is to say that some dimensions are reflections of each other in either direction.

We interact quite freely with different species that are emotionally and mentally compatible. There is a great deal more blending of communication and help than you might think. This is done through love because at our core we are the same. There are degrees of separation but conflict has no part in any thought patterns. We share technology and energetic understandings but where does energetic resonance end and technology begin? To what degree is a walking stick or a wheel a form of physical intervention or help? You do not consider them to be technology because you judge them lowly against some other great advancement.

You are very hung up on spirituality being only mind and heart – that is not so because everything is interwoven. You were also thinking that the finer or higher the vibrations and the more evolved a spirit being, the less need they would have for technology. That somehow the higher mind would have its true power and need nothing else. You have in part understood that arkarnas are conscious programs, but even these can be enhanced by technical intervention.

Antemedi told you the Andromedans use technology on the outer edges of their craft and biospheres to filter out negative emotional energies and thought patterns. When they come across such energies, they do not need to encounter them just because they are there. It's also easier for them to walk on your planet using some degrees of filtering. They can do it without and the technology doesn't have to be used, but is it not easier to walk up a steep mountain with a walking stick than without one?

**R:** Thank you for correcting my conceptions of higher vibrational realms. It's just I thought the higher the realm the more ethereal and the less like humanity they would become.

**O:** *(Speaks directly to me)* Well the mantoids are less man-like! But I take the point of your inner thinking. Moving through 'needing nothing', 'wanting nothing' seems as though it may end in a realm very unlike humanity. Some of the different ways of thinking that we have put forward might imply that. Let us proceed.

**R:** *A tight energy like a wide elastic band has been put around my head and I can now hear the mantoids directly or just more clearly through Orlacka.*

**M:** Because we look so strange doesn't mean we have no love. Yes, we are very different but surely we can be equal in your eyes? You do not know us or the way that we live nor how we treat others and ourselves. You are certainly not in a position to validate yourself to us or use any form of crude comparison system.

**R:** *They give me one of the small spheres to hold. Surprisingly it's very heavy and it seems to slow down the moment of now, but I suspect that's just a feeling when actually the vibrations are getting faster. As they move closer, they tell me my resonance is mingling with theirs. At this point, I fall asleep.*
On waking, I think directly to Orlacka "You are a ninth-density being utilising light as a source and yet these twelfth-density beings appear in what seems to be a lower form projection." *(That thought was rather silly because my prejudgements had overcome love and rationality to the point I had forgotten that they would know everything I was thinking.)*

**M:** Would you wish us to show a different appearance, perhaps one that might accord with your idea of a higher dimensional being? We can change our appearance to you if you wish. Remember you initially saw us as sylph-like gentle humanoids. We are showing our heritage through some of our expressional forms. Do not be deceived by our appearance and misconceptions viewed against your earth idea of insects. There are several dimensional projections of humanoid mantis, you happen to be talking to us on this one. Orlacka has brought you to us to help break down some of your more rigid expectations. Come hold my hand. I will introduce you to some of our elders (as you might think of them).

**R:** *(The scene)* There are lots of strange noises and many mantoids reach out to touch me as we move forward. It's clear what Orlacka first said was more to make me feel comfortable with them than the other way round.

Apparently, they seem unfazed by what I emit as if somehow it delights them to share in another's energy. It's not sexual or erotic but they are clearly enjoying it as a different experience. A most peculiar direct connection so uninhibited – I am totally exposed and vulnerable but the love and trust allow it to sit easily!

I find myself seated in front of what I perceive as an elderly mantoid, maybe someone to whom they defer or respect. Perhaps it is their order of things.

**Mantoid elder (ME):** I see you have come far and travelled with one of your soul partner aspects. Our energetic make-up is different from yours. It could be said that in our evolution we faced very few trials and tribulations in order to vibrate in this dimension. In part that is down to creating very few negative residual energies for ourselves, which we would have subsequently needed to transform. Your energetic make-up is more diverse. It is not better or worse but more diverse.

From your point of view, I can see that you feel a more diverse experience is greater than one than which is not. If it's about memories and an abundance of success badges – then that is so, but they have no currency here. Perhaps you need to acknowledge that much of your experience is repetition in a different form.

If someone passes through schooling without faltering should they be less valued than a pupil that struggles and eventually succeeds? That is to say, there is greater value in striving from failure rather than being focused and unwavering in the lessons of light.

You might say that experience has got you to the levels that you have, and it has. But did it need to be like that, did you need to suffer so much? Suffering may be a part of life for you, but it is not a prerequisite. You do not have to accept it in order to move through it and then not have it by letting go of it. I can understand your races seeking such diversity. But yours is like flipping a coin to see one of the two sides. You carry on to see if the proportion can change to something other than 50/50. Even if it were possible, it would be a pointless experience from our perspective.

Yet as a race here we are – we are not bound by duality or time. This level and our perspectives are similar to many others. We are at a level where it matters not how you got here or what you did or will do – none of that matters. I can see and know you. You think what I am saying is of little significance and meaning. You felt the same for Orlacka's observer outlook before you experienced the outcomes. It is just that you cannot comprehend our ways and us.

**R:** I take your point and will follow your lead.

**ME:** We are not stupid nor can we be fooled. We can see what is – we have achieved this in a different way to you and your kind. We have a knowledge that some aspire to have and this stands us apart from the seekers. Our knowledge is gained through a less tainted approach to the light.

We are a very peaceful race, though our appearances may

say otherwise to you. I might look like a figure of hierarchy as if 'to give the lead'. I am not dominant or indomitable, it is your interpretation of a different social structure. I speak my mind and you think I do so without concern for its impact?

What is there to be offended about and who needs to take it? Offence only exists through a fragile ego-self or not understanding the true sharing of information in frankness. Do not give more value to me as a person because I am the one that speaks. That would be to say no depth of wisdom could exist in a quiet or mute person. Often it is the contrary. I have said my piece, what say you now to me?

**R:** Thank you for your candour I am not offended by what you say. I see your observations exist without the need for value and I like your plain speaking.

**ME:** Good – then may I continue?

**R:** Yes, please.

**ME:** For us, you are a quizzical race. We are aware that deception can be accepted as part of life when it bears no service to the manipulator or the receiver of it. Some of your people seem unaware of what that creates and what they ultimately have to re-experience in energy. For those that are aware, is it acquiescence? Or do others truly not care that they hurt themselves?

**R:** It may be true for a few but not all humans are like that. Our arkarnas have been sabotaged and interfered with. What of you, sir? What gems of your realms or pearls of wisdom do you think can be shared for our benefit?

**ME:** I was sharing my observations – do they not help?

**R:** I see what you say – look at ourselves before we can see another, otherwise we are blind to them. And that last thought is that yours or mine?

**ME:** Does ownership of a thought have any soul offers an alternative view and we adopt it in thinking, should we hail them, should we thank grateful to them?

**R:** What about acknowledge them?

**ME:** Why? Do they need it; are they not comfortable in giving all that they have to all? They are the extension of all and only give to themselves. We give no accolades they have no value.

**R:** You have nothing of value. That concept has been explained to me before, but I slipped into an old way of thinking. Love has no value it can't be valued. You are indeed very different from us. You said, "They are an extension of all"; is that a matter of 'a unitary mind', a 'collective' or a 'hive' mind?

**ME:** You believe you are individual thought, but you choose not to recognise your collective consciousness in every moment. Whereas we accept we are collective with individuality.

**R:** Very interesting and very true.

**ME:** It can be no other way, we have no deceptions.

**R:** To your previous point we have a social etiquette where we thank one another. It is pleasant when someone thanks me when I am not searching for it and it is also a part of our courtesy.

**ME:** Why do you need to thank yourself for giving to yourself? There is no me in that sense of separation – other than I am a part of what is. In any case, what is courtesy? A protocol for saying you appreciate.

**R:** But I can appreciate what I do for myself.

**ME:** Why – why move from one state to another – do you not love yourself all of the time?

I am no nearer to seeing
s that gap is too wide for

l shower you with some
you are one thing and the
hat are you if you are not
What if every day for a
different; who would you
dy different you would, in
ent bodies.

You have already been told you are nobody otherwise you could not be here interacting with these thoughts. You are no body – that could be no energetic body (because energy and body are the same). I could say you are 'nobody in particular'. In your world that would be an insult yet, it's meaning to us is 'you have no particular body and no body as well'.

In that way, you do not belong to something – not even to yourself. I could say that I do not belong here and that would be true – I do not belong anywhere. This is what you would see as a 'freedom from belonging' this would be 'an enlightenment'. But you have already been told freedom is an illusion. How can you belong to something you like or don't like? I am repeating concepts you have heard before in different ways.

But there is another edge to this – 'no edge'. All paradoxical elements come to a point where they have no relationship to each other unless you wish that they do.

This you wish in order that they give you a path or backdrop upon which to see and compare. I am *form* and *not form* – I cannot be compared. In order to see the magnitude of ways that you cripple yourselves, you may wish to read again what I have just said.

A while back Orlacka talked of leaving herself in the past

206

and the future as a perpetuating program. She stated that she was not evolving. What did you think would come after that?

**R:** Nothing or certainly nothing that could be measured. To me, it feels like you don't have pleasure and that doesn't seem like a good evolution or being what you want.

**ME:** Well that depends on what you want and what you find nutritious. That is the only word of yours that I can say for our state of being. Curious perhaps, but we have no need to follow our curiosity or to nurture or feed it. We are not simple creatures who move from one state to another and if we did, it would not be without awareness.

**R:** Using your terms and words I would say, "You are curious to me, but unlike you, my curiosity drives me forward to know more about you."

**ME:** So that is an emotion-led driver system. What will make curiosity satisfied? When will it have done enough? Has it ever done enough?

**R:** So what are your motivators? Interesting, I can see your involvement in returning my thought to me. In my prejudgement, I am expecting you to say you have no drivers because you are so different and almost the opposite of me!

**ME:** I wouldn't say something just because it's the opposite – I would only say what is true – and in this instance, your prejudgement is true to me. I have no motivation, or should I say I have no need for motivation – to do or even just to be.

**R:** Whoa! That sounds like teetering on the edge of existence.

**ME:** I did say that there was no edge.

**R:** Good grief you are either very clever with your words or you know mine in advance – perhaps you have given them to me before I am able to use them.

**ME:** Am I now more interesting than you thought I would

be? Even your thoughts above – your realisations and postulations – they have no belonging. Perhaps it is all that you say and none. What if there is no edge of existence and what if nothing mattered?

**R:** Back to The Boy, the Beast and the Nothingness that Antemedi dictated to me?

**ME:** No, that was you accepting you are presently a series of reflections in duality. Fine that you have seen it, but you do not nccd to keep looking at it to remind you that you are a reflection of your thoughts. When you no longer need reminding, you can accept you are nothing in human duality. That is another step – I would say that is neither backward nor forwards. You have progressed no more forward here than you were before you started. Because – absolutely nothing matters – there is no value.

I know you have been told that before. However, accepting that you can exist without motivation – exist without everything, means you have no edges. You become a different mathematical shape. The mathematics of no-shape, no-form and no relationship to anything else. At these points you don't have concepts of the all nor feel that you are it. There is no realisation that you are the all. Instead, you know you have always been that way without question or observation.

I can assure you it is a very different way of 'being the all' and oneself to anything that you have ever encountered. There are no divisions, there is nothing between anything – no separation. I am all – I am arkarna – interactive with all but not needing to or desiring to. I have no desire – I can be nothing else other than the all.

**R:** I have nothing to say. I am getting some of the feelings you are wrapping me in. As you say, it is different from 'being', it is 'not being' at the same time. The 'not being' is something that goes against every fighting fibre to be something. With that, I realise we are back to your previous words of be *some-thing*. I now see them in a different light. You are a most unusual entity. If I were not introduced in the way I was, I could have misconstrued you as being some other form of deity.

**ME:** Who do you think you are interacting with?

**R:** Ah!! If I follow your teaching – should say myself?

**ME:** Good, but I would say 'myself' does not exist. That is your 'myself', and my 'myself' has no sense of self.

**R:** Wow! when you say such things they come to me with an intense, overwhelming energy. It's taken a lot of explanation to understand and accept what you are saying. I just hope anyone reading this will feel some of the same feelings.

**ME:** I have led you in and you have followed – you, like many others, follow such paths. I know some will feel what you feel when they follow your words – they will feel some of the energy that I am and we all are.

**R:** To follow your thoughts – it should not matter if anyone else were to feel those feelings, but I was so overjoyed I desired it for others.

**ME:** Yet, you are not overjoyed now?

**R:** That moment has passed. Perhaps too much analysis or even the thought of explaining it closed that arkarna from me.

**ME:** That is so and quite correct. If you wish to evolve within loving arkarnas for the right reasons, then one day you will find yourself at such a place as this. What was once sustainable as life or being, then becomes unsustainable. It is neither one nor the other or all – something not fleeting either.

**R:** And there is more of the Isness?

209

**ME:** Is it complete? It cannot be complete or incomplete. It is beyond even that. But yes there are other dimensions different to this one. They are not more evolved, they cannot be. I have no point of reference that would be able to compare this part of me to those other dimensions for you. I cannot be referenced. I can be referred to perhaps from areas such as yours that believe they can reference things – and that they do. They have their references and that suits them till it doesn't.

**R:** So you are not a twelfth-dimensional progression represented by some mantoid experiences.

**ME:** I am and I am not – they are labels. Orlacka had this in her mind bringing you here in order to break your ties and bonds to reference points as human. To show you that there are other 'being experience types', who vibrate to other-dimensional realities and arkarnas. I have had several but what I have said about the difference between mantoid and human experiences of sufferance are still true.

**R:** Thank you. Is there anything I can do to help or show gratitude in any way.

**ME:** I have already given my perspective on 'thank you'. Hold my hand and forever in your heart know that you know me. It is not even a statement that you will – or you always will. You do.

**R:** Again the feeling is overwhelming. Orlacka shows me the way out and as we move through the same crowd I know that in holding the 'elder's hand' I am in fact holding all of their hands. Perhaps that's why I felt the unusual feeling of being touched by so many inquisitive hands on arrival. Though now, the feeling goes somewhat deeper than it did that first time.

# SEVEN

Orlacka returns Robert to a childhood distortion to release a hidden thought to protect himself and others by forgetting and ignoring entity contact. Orlacka shows how that formed a small doubt and an awareness that something was missing. This impacted upon his reflections about the meeting with the mantoids.

**Robert:** I was not aware of the mantoids until your introduction, so I researched them on the Internet. I am a little disturbed by some comments that describe them as negative and manipulative.

**Orlacka:** Some of the lower dimensional mantoids are like humans; is that a problem?

**R:** It's not good to give contrary information to make them out as benevolent.

**O:** It is not the wrong information. There are different insect races and different levels of them. The ones I introduced you to have not been involved in abduction or mistreatment.

**R:** So why don't they do something about it? Surely they have the power?

**O:** Why don't you do something about humanity's mistreatment of other animals and other humans? You have the power!

**R:** It's not the same.

**O:** Oh, so humanity is a special case? It imposes itself on other beings for its own gain.

**R:** Okay, I accept your point, but wouldn't we be leaving the wrong impression.

**O:** What is wrong with saying the truth? Some insectoids undertook a path of peace and love. Things are not always black and white. If the universe took that view of humanity, it would have been consigned to the trashcan long ago. Soul life is about self-determination, self-appraisal and the choice to be what you believe you are. That shouldn't be interfered with.

**R:** Well, we were interfered with and negative entities had an impact on us.

**O:** You are presently unaware that suffering was part of a choice that humanity made. That may be hard to accept, but these are interactive experiences, just like man's terrible treatment of other men, women and children. Don't forget, humanity devolved to the lowest dimensions in order to have those lowly experiences. It is now having the experience of escaping them. Within you, I see the pride you have in working yourself away from negative energies and oppression. These glimmers of pride exist, even though you wish it were not so.

I took you to a particular group of mantoids to show you their life ethos. They have no need for pride or other human desires – those would be seen as encumbrances. They live in joyousness, neither seeking it or not. They have no need to move away from it in order to have the pleasure of regaining it. This has been a challenge for you. This is part of evolution on the road to not evolving that I explained before. I have some other entities I should like to introduce you to – are you happy to proceed?

**R:** Not sure, to be frank.

**O:** Doubts of your own become doubts about what I say. Look into my face, and as I put my hands on your shoulders you can do the same with me. In this way, we will make a good energetic connection. Be steady in my energy; I am taking you to someone you know.

**R:** *(The scene)* We walk over and I find my deceased father digging vegetables with his reduced-size spade, worn down through years of use. He has worked up quite a sweat, having turned over a lot of soil.

**Malcolm (M):** There is a lot of satisfaction that can be had from simple tasks. I get exercise and a sense of achievement.

**R:** *(At this point I see that Orlacka has changed her appearance to that of a young woman – a past girlfriend of mine that my father knew. He gestures to her.)*

**M:** Your friend here has told me all about the communication work you are undertaking. It's good to see you are not bound by society's expectations. It was rather different in my day; expectations were much tighter. It's not surprising that others 'judgemental finger-pointing' and my inability to talk about feelings made me very stiff and reserved. I just wanted to say well done and don't let anything stand in your way. Live to your truth.

**R:** I thank him. We talk a little more and, after a hug and a tear he fades away. I say to Orlacka, "Why were you disguised as that young woman who died many years ago?"

**O:** She was a soft and gentle girl, and your father remembered her as being like that. Her demeanour reminded your father of his sister, who died when he was a boy. Both she and your ex-girlfriend had short human lives. It is a period of sadness he resonates with and, in part, that made him who he was. It is something he is currently working through.

**R:** But you took her image.

**O:** My arkarna had interacted with your father's higher self

213

and it desired to superimpose the young girl's image upon me – it made him most comfortable. He would not have been at ease with my normal appearance. It was a past connection to what was a comfortable time of life when you were a teenager and he was much happier. Emotions of the self are tied to events, and he chose a pleasant era rather than one when he was emotionally unwell.

**R:** But you were happy to take her image!

**O:** She was happy to share it – she is here.

**R**: *(I will call her X to respect her family's anonymity.)*

**X:** I am much better now – I have it in mind that I can change resultant energies from events of the past. If the situation arises and you meet my family again, please be open and candid about what I have said. I would like them to know what I feel. As some of them get older, they will become more reflective on mortality. They will ponder more about death and how I am doing in my mind and heart. I wish them to know what I became. What I was then is no longer the same version of me now.

**R:** I shall not seek them, but if the situation presents itself then I will speak openly with them. *(She thanks me and leaves)*

**O:** Nice young lady, much willingness to learn. Look at me again so we can go to the past of you that needs to be seen.

**R:** *(The scene)* Orlacka takes me to my childhood bedroom where I can see myself under the bed covers hiding from 'the other people' (i.e. her and other spirit guides at the time). We come into the room in a swirling portal arriving at the foot of the bed. Despite what we say to the 'young boy me', he is still frightened of us. I am a little perplexed because, after all these years, I thought I had dealt with those boyhood emotions.

The only way to reach him is by being him inside his head. I reassure him that I am his thoughts and there is nothing to fear. But he doesn't want to listen because I am imposing upon his thoughts. So instead, I sit opposite quietly in reflection. After a while he accepts the fact I mean no malice and gradually stirs out of bed to put his little hand on me, "It's okay, it will get better – they keep telling me that all the time. The other people say it's all right to believe they are real. But I am frightened to believe in case no one believes me.

"Dad says I'm silly, there is no one in the bedroom. I can't tell him any more because he will worry about me and he has too many worries of his own. The best way to help him is to keep quiet and tell the people to go away. They say when they go away it will still be okay and there will be nothing to fear, but I don't believe them. If I don't believe in them then they will have to go away."

I thank that young part of my mind-programming for trusting and speaking up at last. It was an invaluable insight for my adult mind to see that particular child perspective. I have at last been able to see the reasons for *keeping things to myself* – it wasn't the fear of the people at the end of my bed, but what it would do to Dad if I spoke up. I had to protect him because no one else could.

There is a release of energy and we blend together. This event always felt a little obscure, I knew there was something I could not remember or did not want to. I didn't realise that part of my child psyche had kept it to myself and it was still there in that *way* of thinking. In keeping a secret in my childhood self I had kept it from the rest of me for all my life.

**O:** There is a lot you did not realise at the time. This was so you could have the experiences you did. This was an early attempt *to suffer for someone else, thinking it would make them feel better because it seemed the only way you could help them* It became a working part of your subconscious. It is common to many

215

and still exists within the arkarna programs of earth.

Your summation was correct and your subconscious doubted if this episode was true. Because it was linked to protect others and keep things to yourself, it became a kernel of wisdom that could not be touched or seen because it was protecting others – including you. It became a paradoxical conundrum and a prison. You do not doubt us anymore and you no longer doubt. What is – is.

**R:** Thank you.

**O:** Good we can explore more – see how that small piece of hidden doubt made you doubt and question a wonderful and uplifting experience with the mantoids. So where to next – more of your impaired beliefs or the worlds beyond them? It is worth noting that you had a slight deflation in expectations when you were presented with your old childhood subconscious. That was because you placed a higher value upon the meaning of the upper ethereal potentials we show you than those of self-awareness.

**R:** Truth and incisiveness as always, thank you.

**O:** There are many levels at play here. This book is about communication and what is alien or unknown. While there are still unknowns of yourself, that does not stop the progress of what we write. It shows how even the smallest of value systems impacts upon self-communication as well as external communication. So what we bring comes in the truth of what we see – importance has nothing to do with that truth.

As I stand before you – you can see me in my glory. I have no other word that you would understand. Unfortunately, glory can be imbued with a sense of relativity or greatness. Not so; but by the light in me that shines, so do I share what I have freely, without encumbrance or caveats.

So I welcome all who read these words.

**R:** *(Orlacka shows me a glowing sphere cupped in her hands. I can see another world within it. Threads of light dance outwards waiting to connect with me.)*

**O:** Explorations of inter-dimensionality have shown the concept of 'separation of conscious awareness within the same soul self'. I wish to help with that. Allow your energy – the very essence of you to merge with mine and explore deeper with me.

**R:** *(I wonder if I am to enter the ball of light she holds, but the reverse seems to happen and her energy enters me. I feel that she has become me. I am exceptionally calm though a little disjointed because I feel the same threads of energy in my head that were in the sphere.)*

**O:** You will require a short sleep because I need to take you much deeper. When you reawaken in earth consciousness, I will help you re-experience your other states of mind.

**R:** *(I instantly zonk out and return within a few minutes.)*

**O:** On earth, there is much hidden within the corridors of power. Some that stride through those areas know the inner workings of the mind and how it can be manipulated. Energies not within general human awareness have been at play for a long while. Not all man's thoughts came from his current level of self. While you are caged you believe freedom exists because it is part of your 'now program' and distractions create your apparent normal.

We would like to help by taking people out of their current mindset. This is another reason why we are showing those possibilities in this communication. Human potential can be expanded when you communicate with your unknown-self. Unless you experience something different, then there is little or no awareness of other possibilities. Fear can restrict movement, but there is coming a time when people will be fearful of remaining how they are. People will begin to

217

understand that 'the way of thinking' is part of a control system.

**R:** This topic was covered earlier.

**O:** Indeed, but this is deeper. We talked about freedom and being free from the need to be free. One of the constraints to a free mind is a program placed within your collective consciousness, which maintains the status quo. It keeps you from changing the way you think. Instead, you have the appearance of change, of which we spoke before.

Stepping outside of oneself sounds quite radical as if you are leaving the safety of yourself behind. In reality, it is leaving behind your own shackles.

**R:** I can't see how you are going to do that in a few words.

**O:** You do not have my perspective or wisdom. But what is *true change* and do you know what you are changing from?

**R:** This is a repetition of what you have said before – know yourself before you can change yourself or know another.

**O:** But the inevitable progression of your summary will say, "To fully understand another way or person will require you to leave yourself and to become the other person." To 'not be yourself' is a way of changing the way to look around you. When everyone begins to accept they have inter-dimensional states of consciousness, it widens their horizons. When they see their existence has speed restrictors and vibrational mufflers, would they not want to cast them aside?

**R:** Yes but it's one hell of a jump to 'not be oneself'. It's like relying on the hope that a heavy juggernaut travelling at speed will turn itself around when the wheel, the engine management system and the driver are all part of a manipulated program.

**O:** That also depends on what can be seen through the

windscreen – which choice of reality you see and how it's interpreted.

This subject I have introduced is in its formative stages and your interpretations are not helping. The actual experience is so much better, so let's clear the landscape.

**R:** *(The scene)* Things seem to slow down and Orlacka waves her hand slowly in a big arc. Her energy creates a new landscape in front of us. We are standing on a flat plane with nothing in any direction. As we walk forwards, I become aware of a ceiling or plane above. The upper and lower planes seem to be connected on the horizon. We continue walking but instead of the horizon constantly extending forwards it comes into view.

As we get closer to it the plane we are standing on begins to disintegrate. The energy of it flows upward like an inverted waterfall. It feels as if we are looking through the back of a waterfall to something ahead of us. Where we stand makes everything feel like it's a 'replication' or a reflection of the plane above. Our ability to know this only exists where the two planes meet. The 'awareness of replication' is also changing the planes. They can no longer sustain what they once were.

The horizons to our sides and rear and begin to shrink and what was great distance is no longer. The plane that we were standing on and the one above begin to meet one another and shrink the area that we can occupy. A crescendo of light and a loud roaring noise encircles us. I become aware of my limitations and repetitions – what were my limited horizons are no longer. My only choice is to move forward with Orlacka into the waterfall of energy between the planes. In doing so I become separated from what was and I no longer have any desire to return to it (see book cover image).

The energy we are moving through is most invigorating. As

we step further into it, I feel that I am walking in all directions. Like being in the centre of a circle splitting into 360 degrees and walking in each direction at the same time. Front or back seems to be twisted. It's a very new feeling and I am struggling to cope with the eye-information feed from all directions.

**O:** The energy will move around your back and then to your front where it will pour into all your chakras and out at the back of them. You will be able to see that your whole body becomes a torus with many sub-torus or vortex fluctuation points. To see yourself as energy is to know the nature of soul. This space may be as small or large as you wish. Other people may enter and interact with you. All that is here is you. Exceeding contextualisation beyond the need for concepts will allow the soul to show itself to you. It shows itself to itself.

**R:** It's quite a light show! *(Orlacka shows me the same sphere as before cupped in her hands).*

**O:** Do you wish for more of the same? Do you wish to move forward by questioning me – with questions that create parameters? Or do you wish to step away from self and see what comes with no conditions?

**R:** So many times you say this and so often I fall back to the default position – humanity's definition of 'the way to think'.

**O:** We shall say no more on the matter and I hope not to remind you so often. Let my thoughts become yours as if they are yours. You have no need for doubting yourself or have concern for slipping. Doubt will ensure that you slip back.

How you presently hear is an extension of soul self. Do not question yourself, instead observe your thoughts and your mind. Look without judgement or discernment and see what soul brings you. There is no need to filter thoughts – you know what you need and you only need to observe. I have used the word you and not higher self or soul because all of you is equal to yourself. It is possible to complicate 'observation' with discernment. It is easier without, then there is nothing in the way.

Despite your protestations and questions, we are able to bring you new realisations. The more we do this, the more your program will change and you begin to observe and not react. Observation does not require action.

You wonder – how will you know when observation has provided its fullness? That is something you cannot question, as that will restrict it. It will be what you allow it to be.

There is no reckoning in observation – nothing should exist between you and what you observe. Most of all, nothing should exist between you and yourself if you are to observe yourself. You are what you observe and focus exists in all things.

So – what can you bring to yourself that you have not before?

If I say there was nothing to observe that sounds as though there is nothing more to see. But it is your *'act of observing'* – you think this is how to do it but observing is neither an act nor a doing or thinking of doing. That's why observing felt so odd and detached in the experiential 'horse metaphor'.

Within that unencumbered mental space, we can observe one another because other-selves are 'our self', of course. We have nothing to gain or lose from this; everything is here and nothing is missing. It is a matter of free access and the awareness that you have free access. 'You cannot know' until you do, so there's no sense in trying to see what's here for all the reasons we have repeated; that's the old way which is trying to be an observer and not being it.

Allow yourself to feel my body movements and my

demeanour. Walk forward into me and become the observer within me.

**R:** *(The scene)* I am within her. I feel the soft flowing blue robes with energetic yellow trimmings. Her energy is golden and it wafts in soft gestures like slow, gentle hand movements. An energetic belt at her waist holds the inner tunic in place, the remainder of the garment stops at knee level. Floppy silky trousers swish back and forth as we walk forwards. She pushes open a dark grey-black padded door. Hinged on the right it opens in front of us 'at her thoughts'.

We enter a much larger room and in the distance, figures are silhouetted in front of pale yellow lighting. Many of the Arcturians are dressed similar to Orlacka, but some have purple and gold or emerald green and gold energetic robes. Apparently, it's not a dress code as such but an energy manifestation into apparel. As I inspect the garments more closely, they seem to have other colours within them. The green contains red and yellows and the purple is red and blues, whereas the blue has pinks and a myriad of smaller coloured energy threads. I am entranced just looking at the light show in the garments that pass me by. Orlacka regains my concentration on what she wants to show me.

There are several groups of Arcturians who surround various speakers standing on small podiums or platforms created by thought. Energetic threads are linking the people in the groups with each other and the speakers that they gravitate to. It's clear to see that information is being shared among them.

As we walk in further, we are acknowledged by people who know Orlacka. I could not have done this by myself because there is a 'complexity' of energy, which contains information that seems indecipherable to me. After a short while, we walk up and onto a large stage and join others who are already standing there. A quietness falls over most of the people and the energetic threads connecting them become steady as they fluctuate less. They orientate concentration to look at the main stage where we stand.

There is a variety of energies within the crowd, some have more vibration than others. The ones looking less bright do not have their full consciousness with them but they are downloading information in energy form that can be processed later. It's interesting to see the arkarna programs of these beings interacting and working with each other. At some stage, they might be here in 'more consciousness' in a different moment but at present, it's as if they can still hear and speak as if they were fully here.

The arkarna programs of those who are more present have a different feeling. Because I am within Orlacka, she says I am interpreting this information through her. She assures me that whatever arkarna people are in, it is the same as if they were fully here. She also points out that interactive programs require a deeper explanation but we should not distinguish between consciousness levels. We should interact as if everyone were fully conscious of everything.

The event is all quite matter-of-fact. There are no ceremonies and the speakers have no more importance than the interactive audience. It's more a sharing of information than giving any insight or talk.

Standing within Orlacka, we are located on the left side of this very wide podium. Her energy is swirling and mixing with the others around us. I wonder if this how our human thoughts look because we don't see the energy of them. She still has the 'energetic orb' cupped in her hands. Five similar beings stand on our right. She raises the orb in her right hand at the same time as the others raise theirs. The energy vibrations of all six orbs connect with each other. Threads flow from the orbs to the participants below. The energy of the audience returns making a heightened vibrational resonance. It is an enormous feeling of expansion with a powerful inter-connectedness. One of the beings that is two down from us on the podium starts speaking.

**Podium voice (PV):** "All gathered here today in whatever form or whatever dimension, be you at one and let one be with you. I speak for the group of six souls – we wish to share experiences with you. If our energies are compatible, let them be at one with you. Let us be as we are – one and all together"

**R:** *(The scene)* The hands of the six come back down and the orbs are placed in front of their chests. Purple light streams out joining the six hearts together before it streams out to the participants again. In response, the audience reaches back to us, enabling me to bathe in this feeling of no separation. I know full well that I can only do this by residing in the experience of Orlacka.

**PV:** "We all come to share in the wish that others may benefit from our separate thoughts and experiences. We are all aware that there are many planes and many ways in which to experience them. Light to light and like to like. Everyone from any world can travel to be with us. We share with open hearts so others may see from our perspective that which is unknown to them. That which is yet to come is that which has been – the past and future are expressions of belief. We have tenderness and awareness for our soul connections in lower vibrational domains."

**R:** *At this point, Orlacka quietly explains that it is a very short delivery but she is conveying a much longer interpretation to me so I can understand.*

**PV:** As 'one' we have a duty of 'one' to be as 'one' to think as 'one'. Remember our hearts do beat as 'one' while we experience degrees of other soul self. Other aspects of our soul do not do our bidding to give us experience. Free will exists within consciousness separation. We cannot be imbued or enhanced by our souls' actions in those domains – betterment has no purpose to us. Our souls are one while they are not and yet there is no difference in what we are – it is as if we are still one. Separation is only an aspect of the soul, it is a program and an illusion.

The six of us standing here have enhanced the vibrations of our other soul-selves. They are not aware of our capabilities or of what we are to them.

We do this for our lower soul-selves because they are us. They feel separate from us though we have no such feelings. We do not experience the intensity of their struggles. Today, we have enhanced their energies and it is not often that we have six aware consciousnesses capable of being in the same vibration as us.

**R:** *Orlacka and the five other Arcturians step back from the other lower vibrational entities like me. I am no longer inside Orlacka.*

I feel intense sadness, separation and vulnerability. Everyone can see everything in me; there is nowhere to hide my thoughts or deeds. But as I become more attuned with the unconditional love, it calms and extinguishes those feelings. I am aware of chatter forming in my head. There are many participants communicating with me. It seems this level of arkarna can be experienced in different ways and I can be aware of as much of it as I need or want to.

The program is incredible, many are communicating with me at some level and I with them but it's going on without my direct awareness. Yet at the same time, the program allows me to be aware of specific individuals. I have not chosen them but it doesn't seem random, so the program must be highly evolved in order that it gives my soul exactly what I need from an interaction. Without asking or enquiring, it provides exactly what I need because I am a part of it.

One particular Arcturian focus (AF) in the crowd reaches me through the arkarna.

**AF:** Are you fully aware that we know all your types of thoughts? We can also see your events as they will and do unfold. We see them as the timelines of the 'full souls' that stand upon the podium. This is because we are all you and you us. Orlacka could have explained our encounter in advance but that would not have been the same as the current experience. I can see all of you but I do not need to focus upon any part of you in order to know you. Knowing someone is not the same for you as it is for me.

At the moment, in order to know and understand others at this level, you are being helped to join our throng. Because I am at one, I have access to all that I need; we are as one so I have no enquiries of you. You are having an experience with me and while I am not directly connected with your soul, there is still nothing between us.

**R:** Yes this is most heart-warming it's as natural as my own thoughts. At this point, Orlacka returns but keeps her energy partially separated from me. I realise this is to give me a less filtered or enhanced perception. Perhaps it's to allow me to feel my presence here isn't totally dependent on her. We descend into the throng of participants and head towards the way we came in. As we progress, it partly reminds me of the observational touches by the mantoids. As well as me getting knowledge and experience, they gain something by a direct feeling of my energetic presence in this arkarna.

**O:** It's a more of an enhanced contact or a willingness to touch you unconditionally at your level.

We will be meeting a specific group of Arcturians who have

226

an interest in human interactions. We will pass through a couple of doorways, which is my way mentally and physically moving you to a desired space. It is not so much a place as a space that exists in non-locality not subject to time and restrictive mental constructs.

**R:** *(The scene)* We go through another set of padded doors and are immediately greeted by more Arcturians on our arrival. Orlacka energetically removes (mentally changes some of her garments) and she feels less adorned, less formal. Not that formality would be the right description I suppose.

**O:** You suppose correctly.

**R:** *(The scene)* We move to our right and she sits on one of several informal round cushions (cylinder shapes with the circular ends at the top and bottom). Orlacka slants her legs to her right with feet pulled back from her knees. What we might think of as ladylike. She smiles at my thoughts.

**O:** Come, sit next to me. You will be with my energy and therefore able to focus. Look forward – remember you will understand through the arkarna programs as they best interact with you. You will hear the same as the rest of us but only as much as falls within or just outside your vibration.

**R:** *(The scene)* There are several speakers who are on the 'same wavelength'; they walk among those that are seated. They are saying the same things but in different ways. It doesn't feel like a lecture because the audience is interacting through the mental arkarna programs. I begin to hear the projections from one of the orators who is standing a few Arcturians in front of us.

**Orator:** Human expression is an unusual thing. They need to express as individuals and to explain themselves to others in the desire that they may be understood by each other. Some humans suppress their needs because they are bound by fear,

227

and they let others overrule their desire to express. They will have difficulty understanding that our ways of expressing are very different.

For a start, we do not do things in order that we are recognised as worthy individuals. None of that has any significance because we express as oneness – as one beating heart. It is difficult for them to see how an individual can exist in such an environment. Our individuality does not require itself to be seen as an individual. It requires no recognition in order for it to exist or not to exist.

**R:** I think, *That is so poignant and powerful. What he says is so true – all that clatter and noise just to know that we are who we are as humans – clatter and noise – no wonder it has no satisfaction.* The male orator has heard this in me and acknowledges that by looking directly at me.

**Orator:** We have desires that will not be understood by man. We doubt some would be recognised as desires because we are so removed from their ways. However, there is no intention to say that we are remote and separated from them.

**R:** *(Observing)* He focuses on my face and I know that he knows – that I am recording what he is talking about on my laptop.

**Orator:** Your presence and typing is a part of what has happened and is in alignment with my expression within this arkarna.

**R:** *(Observing)* He either places more focus on to me or I am drawn deeper into his arkarna because I can see he is still interacting with others while having a direct interaction with me at the same time.

**Orator:** Is this incisive interpretation by you? Or are you allowing the information to flow to you? If so then that has nothing to do with self – it is instead a function of the oneness upon this plane. So it could be said your ability to 'see yourself' inhibits your understanding of our realm and us. What good is 'yourself' here in the oneness? You would be an outsider – remaining within yourself.

**R:** *(Observing)* I see him focus on Orlacka and I sense they are discussing within their arkarna programs what's the next appropriate encounter.

**Orator:** This will perplex you. Did I already know what was to be said in this moment or did that become influenced by my discussion with Orlacka? If so, was that a change or was it already part of what was due to happen? It might be, that everything you do here with us has already happened and you are accessing it through a set of arkarna programs.

If so, is it the first time for you or is this is just a review of what has already happened? Seeing the 'future of what is to be' or the 'past of what was' does not hold value for us. It does for you because it relates to your frailty within a sense of self. With all this being possible, how then does life exist on these realms? Where and upon what do we put our awareness?

I have said how your understanding of my words will be hampered. One way to overcome this is to disconnect your consciousness from the lower arkarnas. That will disable your current interpretation methods. It's a little like the information that passes straight to your core when you resonate with the energy of a powerful enlightened speech. However, there is no point in giving great insights if it cannot be understood in your context. You may think you understand what has been said but often it is not the same as was intended or actually given. Examples of that exist throughout this dialogue. What is given through any higher arkarna has to be relative to your terminology in order to be understood.

In addition to disconnecting to lower arkarnas, you may

allow yourself to be guided to new ones and the information they have. You have the freedom to think and to ask questions despite their pitfalls. Bringing more consciousness to higher realms adds and expands more of human 'light connection'.

There is now a window to peer through when before it did not exist. It could not be known because your mental radars were not of the frequency to see it or understand it. Each of you will see this, as you desire to experience it. For some, it is an opportunity for others an impossibility and maybe for most, it is just not relevant to earth life.

I am aware that I have not answered the conundrum I placed before you. But I am hoping you can begin to see that it's more about the 'order of awareness' or the 'order of focus' and how the arkarnas give you an experience. For me, position in a sequence is not relevant because that's a determination of the type of experience you wish for. Yours would be the desire for sequential experience because you have the inability to alternate awareness in the many points of focus that you are having at the same time.

You are remembering this realm because it took place in your last night's sleep. Unfortunately, you may see that as a sequential order because your now subsequent full awareness appears at a later stage in your time arkarna. It doesn't have to be in a particular order. You place emphasis on when – when it's not relevant to living within wonderful arkarna programs of multiple interactions. I have no night or day in the same way you do. You need sleep in order to be removed from sequence and encounter other levels of arkarna awareness. You might wonder how that fits in with these levels of collective arkarna. Because time is not relative, it doesn't matter when you interact with this arkarna. Nor does it matter when we interact with others – it's about our awareness of it and there isn't a 'when'. You might think we need not be aware of everything that we do within our arkarna because they are self-propelling programs. But that would be to dismiss arkarnas as function and not entity because you are yet to understand their full nature and glory.

You are not asking questions, so am I talking as I wish? Am I aware of what you would ask and giving you those answers in my next words? How could I do that unless we were 'at one'? You are helping by deciding that 'you are not separate' by way of interpretation. Of course, there are many points that I have not explained to full satisfaction; that is why we are still interacting.

You comprehend some of what I say but you dance around the edge of other understandings. It would help if you could see them more holistically without time and value.

Then I will boldly say that none of this matters – it matters not for a single moment in time, it never did and it never will. Does even understanding have importance? If you can't understand the totality of your soul or the way of the universe it does not stop your function. Nor does it stop you from being whom you decide you are.

Yet even though I have drawn this line in the sand, you still gravitate to the thought, *it would be good if I could understand more*. Distilled to say that the purpose of our conversation is for you to know more.

**R:** Yes, that's how it feels.

**Orator:** You mind trips on an old whisper in the breeze. It is not good or bad to know more or less. You are back to the desire for personal evolution again. Do you require better definitions or their removal? Both of those will inhibit.

**R:** You see the cards I hold in my hands and the edge of new games that I have faltered at.

**Orator:** Then it is only a game. Games have no reflection on value and there is no winning or losing.

Where did the picture of a hand of cards come from? Was it your internal intuition or did I place that thought in order that I could answer it in the way that suited best? Whose thought is whose and when? Does it matter whose it is when it is actually 'not individual' in that sense?

**R:** If I have listened to you correctly, none of that matters. So do answers and questions actually exist for you or is the Mowhar paradox somehow involved?

**Orator:** Questions and answers abandoned. Your own thoughts are on the right lines but are they following my thoughts. Should I say, "Well done for your thinking?" or "Well done for allowing my thoughts to form in you as if they were yours and mine at the same time?" Do not give me credit for this and give it not to you either. Should you say well done for the program that makes the sun rise every morning?

This is the crux of the matter. How do we define you or me or us and our combined thoughts?

**R:** If 'we, the, us' cannot be defined, then can arkarnas be understood?

**Orator:** And, of course, that does not matter, as I have alluded to – but to you it does. Things that defy explanation still require a reason as to why they should be unexplainable. If there is a good reason for 'no answer' then that is the answer. That is to do with your inability to satisfy yourself with the fact that there is no answer.

If all things are from Mowhar – the flux, the dimensions, and the information fields, then so are the ways we use or bend paradox to live within its possibilities, all of which are endless. That is neither an answer nor a good reason, that is about the way you use paradox within a paradox. Unlimited potential extends beyond anything you can currently hold as a concept. Limitlessness exceeds concepts while having none of them at the same time.

If we are to look a little deeper into arkarna programs, we must start from the premise that all things are possible. However not all things need to be made into possibilities no matter how likely or unlikely they are. We could say that is a limiting factor or that those words are part of an arkarna program. It is part of the premise that all things are possible including *not needing some possibilities*. And there we have a basic paradoxical program within the Isness. It would seem sensible to say 'that nothing came before anything else'. But nothing is not even 'non-existence' because that exists by relationship to existence.

We are struggling to use your word 'nothing' for a 'non-concept' that cannot be described in relation to other things or in relation to itself because it does not exist. The phrase 'nothing comes before anything else' is wrong; it cannot come from before because there was *no before*. You do not have a word for 'that which is not'. So imprint upon your enquiring mind that there is only *IS* – and it *IS* all possibility. This is why the Andromedans use the term *The Isness*

**R:** You previously mentioned un-chosen possibility. Can you define it?

**Orator:** It is just what it says.

**R:** So un-chosen possibility is not what wasn't there – 'the nothing' that can't even be a concept, so it must be a part of the Isness.

**Orator:** Correct – But for an understanding of 'un-chosen' we need to look at its relationships within your subconscious minds. Some people believe that which is not chosen is to be feared. As if something evil can exist in the un-chosen lying in wait for anyone making a foolish or innocent choice. For those who think like this, it would be a good reason not to choose the unknown. What they don't realise is they have already chosen fear above all other possibilities. In this way, fear exists everywhere even the un-chosen.

The Isness is all possibilities but not all things are desired into being. It's all a matter of choice within the context of each dimension. The dimensions can ultimately affect one another, but free will on each of them and inter-dimensional soul connections keep vibrations in check. There are no restrictions but arkarna parameters. If you wished to see that as a restriction, you may do so – that is a personal choice of the many options available in your arkarna.

**R:** That's an interesting way to put it – does it mean all arkarna programs are basically the same but the choices we make define our dimensions and adapt the arkarna?

**Orator:** That is part of the reality but the choice to make the arkarna programs in this way was done at the time of their creation. They have in part been adapted, but that was not a matter of when or sequential choices. There are other Mowhars and other universes with variations of arkarna.

We have said that our universe is connected to the rest of itself and non-locality. In addition, there are connections between what was Mowhar and other Mowhars of other universes, some of which function well and some of which did not. They became ideas and no more than that and would have disintegrated. When we look at arkarnas we cannot exclude anything. We need to view them holistically in terms of potential, pulse energy, dimensions and how minds and souls are an intrinsic part of the same system.

Your arkarna, while being holistic, runs on programs adapted to your choices and beliefs. When you choose one particular route or action, that may be seen as a restriction to another. Choices are paradoxical but that's also about the way you chose to see them. Instead of seeing wonderful infinite choices to experience, you have reinforced your arkarna program with thoughts like *What am I restricted from?* The universe answer is *absolutely nothing,* but you will continue to look through restriction unless you alter or upgrade your thoughts. In this way, you would continue to see restriction even though there is none.

Imagine if you could choose everything at the same moment. Not only would there be chaos but no way of understanding the chaos. That would, in effect, be a failed Mowhar – no order and no choice. Choosing everything is a paradox because that's choosing to have everything when you already have it.

There are some very fine subtleties within paradox, so it just goes to show the wonderful nature and the complexity of the amazing arkarnas.

Choice is not restrictive and having multiple experiences is to have multiple lives on different dimensions.

Do not reference any of your feelings to that which is 'un-chosen'; it needs no such reflection. There is no need to be sad for that which did not come into existence – it did not know that it could or that it was not one of your choices. There is no need for that which you do not need. Arkarna programs are beautifully complex but simple at the same time; they would be, they are from Mowhar.

As I begin to conclude, I would like to draw your attention to the constructive use of paradox while living within its unconstructive elements. I would like you to begin to accept that you are an arkarna. It's easy to see that you are 'Robert Arkarna'. You conform to your own rules and programs including the *breaking of rules* because that is one of the rules.

You are a living consciousness of complex programs working on a variety of levels. We could have described this as *soul,* but that would be insufficient because your definition of soul doesn't include its complexity and ability.

Can you see how far you have moved from the initial descriptions of soul at the beginning of this book?

Refer to our holistic description of arkarna and try to see you are the originator of the arkarna programs and the being that experiences them. You are a multifaceted program working on several different dimensions at the same time. This you can conceptualise and accept as the 'current expression of yourself' – you – your soul and your programs – you are one and the same.

However, you are also other arkarna programs, but in order to have your current experience, your awareness of those programs is very limited as they run contiguous with yours.

We experience arkarna differently to you because we are more at one with our multidimensional nature. Neither do we experience you as you experience yourselves. It's a matter of choice and the choices made within the multiple arkarna expressions.

**R:** Thank you, but unfortunately, it seems as if we are back to square one alongside the other descriptions of 'the appearance of separation'. I don't feel much further forward nor that I live within the union.

**Orator:** Despite what you feel, you have seen and taken on board the fullness of a few more paradoxical choices at other arkarna levels. Stop trying to understand through your earth programme 'that which you cannot'. Instead, when you wish or choose, you may be here with us in our arkarna – as one of us. Everything you need is brought into being for you by arkarna, and she is the consciousness of all of us and she is us. You no longer need proof of this – that is constant proof, which is reassurance. Just choose and do not seek proof, as that will distort what you see through it.

**R:** That facet could be added to Antemedi's initial exploration of proof.

**Orator:** Be mindful of my delivery, not a previous one. Imagine and feel that you are me – sense my energy and arkarna as if we are one. I am without frustration because progression and result are not what I choose to see within the multitude of choices. Everything has its place within my mind, within the greater arkarna/me. I have no desire to move you forward – I have no desire to see you evolve. If you could choose to see 'no values', you would indeed be more like this dimension and me.

**R:** And that is the stumbling block, there seems to be a limit to what I can fully understand. *(So, in frustration I stopped typing and walked away for a while – when I came back I immediately fell into a deep sleep. I awoke feeling very relaxed, in a different zone. I re-read what I had written in readiness to start again.)*

**Orator:** When you have frustration you believe you have reached your limit. That is only a feeling and a belief.

**R:** Your feelings don't get in the way like ours do.

**Orator:** That is so they do not. As for you – take all the pain in the following words deep into your heart and feel the intensity of them:
*There is nowhere to go from here – there is nothing more to say – you have reached the limits of your understanding.*

Those words could be a sign of achievement but you see them as a failure. You believe there is a limit to what your arkarna programs can deal with; that is why we tweaked your program when you were asleep. The program that you have now is different because there is a little more energy around; *you have given up on giving up* – another little subtlety in your program. This means there is no trying, no needing, and no wanting to. You are relaxed, unlike before. There is nothing more you can do in the old program. Nothing more you could do as Robert the program.

**R:** True, I am not vexed but that's not giving up on Robert, that's giving up on one of my programs, it's not the same thing.

**Orator:** When is it the same thing? When are you no longer Robert?

**R:** When I die

**Orator:** No! It's when you decide you are no longer Robert.

**R:** That's similar to what's been said before but when there are so many stimuli to the contrary, how is that possible? In any event, I am functioning in an earth arkarna.

**Orator:** All that is so but it is still a matter of choice. Choosing from the Isness of possibilities that is where I came in today. Choices you could not take because they would either create chaos or cancel out other possibilities. In addition, you have choices believed not possible when in fact they are.

**R:** I know what you say is true, but something eludes me.

**Orator:** You elude yourself.

**R:** How do I not? – Our conversation is beginning to sound like Confucius or Yoda, who says the same things backwards.

**Orator:** I hear you, so let me review things in a practical way. Here you sit in your lounge typing on a laptop – you can see inter-dimensional beings. Not only can hear their thoughts but you are cognisant of their true essence. You can discuss and interact with them as if you are in the same time period.

Some of these beings have told you that they are 'you'. They have provided you with experiences and information that is not commonly available. You know you are not psychotic and the only thing you have is a slight struggle with accepting more and more the loss of yourself as Robert.

**R:** Put like that it sounds quite normal. I feel as if I am touching the edge of something tangible that I cannot reach.

**Orator:** Then more of you has to die to be it. I use the word die to show the enormity of what I say. This is not an exercise in jousting with concepts or testing boundaries and theories. This is real – are you to reconcile this? If I were to say it is 'a walk in the park', it would give no gravity to the gravity of what you are doing.

What if we walked along a path in the park and partway through I stopped and turned you around. I could open your eyes to that peaceful transit but then reveal the walk I had hidden – another route on a swaying tightrope spanning a deep crevasse containing 'fears of destruction'. Would a more dangerous walk result in greater meaning and discovery?

It might show foolishness or, alternatively, your faith and trust in me. But you no longer need to test your faith in us, it is beyond question. What value is there in walking new paths through old value systems that test your mettle? You cannot be guided towards yourself by experiencing something different than it really is. That is false pretences for good intent.

The outcome would mean that you had not, in true awareness, reached this place – right here now with me. We could not drag you nor insist, and if we lifted you up without gaining the wisdom, you would fall back again. That is not our way.

**R:** Your words and wisdom have found their marker within me. I am made happy through your wisdom, and I am glad you are all a part of my life as I am of yours. The struggle to be one or the other, or the all, has faded – it just is the way it is and one day it will be another 'just the way it is'.

*(I see part of my previous programming falling away from me. The energy that Orlacka previously cupped in her hands she now places into the centre of my head.)*

**O:** You do not need to react to situations in order to be yourself. Choose who you wish to be regardless of what the stimuli say. Frustration did not need to exist within the process of discovery. Feelings did not need to dictate to you. Frustration is a mere veil to be pulled back easily and discarded – this you did not see.

Keep relaxed and in contact at the highest vibration. You can and we will show you higher pathways.

*(Antemedi appeared a few moments before Orlacka departed.)*

**Antemedi:** Time to leave some of the rarefied levels and return to more practical aspects of communication.

# EIGHT

Antemedi presents some unusual concepts that we might like to accept into our future arkarna programs. Some of these help to remove our anchors in ridged structured thinking. He takes us deeper into the arkarnas of Isness. He and higher levels talk about our imagination and how everything is 'made up' within that.

**Antemedi:** 'As things begin so they will'. It sounds like 'something in nothing', which the Arcturians have pointed it out as an impossibility. We have been through discussions about 'what is a beginning' and what is 'new' or a 'start'. So let's do something different that can 'just be' without the need to clarify it first or see the variable 'ways we think' about it.

**Robert:** That is still an introduction!

**A:** And what's wrong with an introduction? Should I not talk as I walk you through a new doorway?

**R**: *(We enter a busy room with workstations and interactive monitors. He introduces me to Karliene.)*

**Karliene:** Welcome both. Come with me; I have something Antemedi wishes me to show you.
*(He presents an ornamental curved sword secured in a scabbard and places the scabbard sash around my neck – most bizarre and completely out of context.)*

**A:** 'What is – is' were my previous words.

**R**: *(Energy begins to revolve around the sword and sash creating a circle around me.)*

241

**A:** You heard me say 'sword of destiny', but you refrained from typing it thinking it was a mythical object that was not real. If such a thing were true, why would it be presented to you?

I did this to shock and obtain your attention so that you would listen to my words with care. Of course, the sword is a representation, but it showed your unwillingness to type what might look like nonsense or be some egotistical jaunt swelling from the depths. If you look in front of you, we have all sorts of mythical objects made 'apparent'. They are imbued with certain energies. But there is nothing magical or mystical about them. Their appearance is only a portrayal of the energy that exists here.

Over time your histories have told of such powers. Humanity had no way of explaining or understanding how these energies came into being. It was easier to interpret and depict them as mythical objects. Do you think objects like this are no longer needed because we have provided explanations for mental and energetical prowess?

Are the metaphors we used in our explanations so different from the ancient sagas with amulets and talismans, representing forces of goodwill? The horse metaphor could have been likened to Pegasus. Orlacka's energy orb could be compared to a crystal ball with inter-dimensional aspects. Energies of chakras can be shown in patterns, dress code and jewellery. If an amulet is supposed to possess powers, how deep does the belief in it need to be in order for the amulet to imbue its power? Is the object the power or is it the focus for your belief that creates the power?

These energy explanations are interchangeable and there are connections between all that I have said. I know you think this seems out of context, but what I say is for good reason.

I want to explore further with you 'the power of

acceptance'. It is the place of no doubt existing beyond the need for belief. What is – is. There are no questions about it because when you are there you have no questions. They are answered and not answered in the same moment of paradox. Questions are pointless. There is every point and no point to them. Concepts lose their validity the closer we get to the Isness, its power and potential.

*(Karliene wraps up several talismans into an energy vortex, which gradually expands and engulfs Antemedi and me. There is a great peacefulness. From the horizon, a winged horse moves swiftly towards us. It is symbolic because it is the means by which to travel to other worlds. As it approaches, a space vessel appears on our right.)*

**A:** Which has more power or prowess? The reality of a mystical entity or a spacecraft developed over millennia. What weight do you put on a living machine that has management 'self-aware programs' interacting with our arkarnas?

**R:** I guess it depends on your take on life. Both of these would be quite unbelievable to most people.

**A:** Well you are not most people. I am asking about your perception.

**R:** Well Pegasus, despite being mythical, seems more of an entity whereas the craft, though quite marvellous in its energetic connections, seems a little more mechanical.

**A:** The craft is function and a result of us working and advancing within our arkarna.

**R:** But the horse does not seem to be a function of what you or we could have done.

**A:** You think there is no 'value bias' from where you view and that you are comparing an entity to a 'created form', which will supply our need for travel. But what is form and what is function? What is energy – how should energy represent itself in *form* if it is not to be seen as essence energy? The essence energies cannot be seen by the average human eye so for them they may as well not exist. In order to interact with energy at lower densities, it has to have form and function like the craft.

**R:** Yes, but at whose bidding and whose inventive creation?

**A:** Was not Pegasus created 'for your bidding' in the same way that you create your technology – at your bidding for your purpose? If you had encountered benevolent mantoids in years gone by without recording devices, you could have only explained such beings with carved figures and statues. Verbal traditions would pass through so many generations that the origin would be unknown, and in that way, they would become mythical.

**R:** OK, I gather that you are showing similarities between function and purpose. That mythical objects, beings or stories are an extension of function and form, possibly created for our own purpose of trying to understand or record.

**A:** So how do you know that the mantoids were not a creation of your imagination or of ours?

**R:** Because I trust what I am seeing and what you say; because it's all been beneficial and you have never lied.

**A:** That is true but it is not quite what I meant. We are talking about energies and their representations. The mantoids could have been seen as a type of human-like being. At their essence soul, they are able to take a different form.

**R:** Do you mean, are we are making them up or moulding them in our imagination to fit what we want?

**A:** There is that possibility but it is not so. Let's look at form as a representation of energy. An insect on earth has a form adapted to its environment, but primarily it is an energetic part of an insect self-aware arkarna and a part of the environment and earth arkarna. The form is the best fit for the integration of that energy within the environmental arkarna. So which comes first? Certainly not the chicken or the egg! It will always be the energetic intent, which interacts with the energetic program of the environment.

The insects provide a valuable input into the totality of the environmental function. The arkarna 'nature life' programs can change very quickly or over long periods, this is then perceived as physical evolution. It is the same with humanoids and mantoids. There are different arkarna programs across the universe that give rise to a wide variety of beings. Naming a mantis as a mantoid is to align it with your humanoid soul nature and not a hive of ants.

**R:** Yes, but this doesn't square with your question – how do we know that the mantoids were not a creation of your imagination or ours?

**A:** In part, that's to do with your interpretation of the word 'imagination' it being imaginary made up and not real. What I am trying to bring you to is a better acceptance and understanding of creative thought beyond the need to believe. We touched on this with 'creative thinking'.

**R:** Are you saying, because we are all interconnected, it means the mantoids are a creation of us and we of them.

**A:** That is in part true but not what I wanted to bring to you. Inspect an apple in your mind and look at where the red colours intermingle with the greens. There are degrees and areas of blending. However, the mind tends to see the red and the green sections and not often the mix. You could look at thousands of apples but your mind imagines 'the red-green split' without much blending even if it's not what your eye perceives as light. In part, you imagine what you see or expect to see.

Now then – is that a true image or not? Putting this 'in' your mind is the same as putting an 'in' after the 'g' of image; it makes the word 'imagine'. In the case of the apples, your mind distorts or creates what you see in your mind. It is not necessarily a true eye image. In which case what you imagine and what you image are both a function of the mind. Energy has form and you can select how you view the image. If it brings what is needed then why get hung up on what you see?

**R:** Because I would prefer to see what's projected rather than putting my interpretation upon it.

**A:** But you always do – that's how interpretation works.

**R:** We have moved away from 'creative thought' existing beyond doubt and the need to believe.

**A:** It's all part of the same subject – creative imagination. When you have created something from your imagination you give it form from the energy of thought. You allow images to come into your head and muse upon them, rolling them around looking at them from several positions, and then you paint them in oils on canvas.

**R:** Yes, but they are not real they might be concepts or feelings, not real places (though some are).

**A:** And that is what you portray – concepts and feelings that come into your mind from yourself. What is real? We have constantly reminded you about the information fields, harmony and pulse. We are entering a different energetic space, but you are bouncing off its edges and not passing into it. We are getting closer to another aspect of the Isness and creativity – the use of energy to create form without doubt or belief.

That statement seems an extraordinary possibility for you. So much so that it has appeared as a tiny smudge of doubt, which you haven't detected yet. But I can see it because the possibility now exists to create both negative form as well as positive form from energy.

Dispense with that thought; it is only a doubt do not give it energy. Only by clear thinking can you enter these arkarnas of Isness.

The reason I talked about the mantoids is because they live and work from this aspect of the Isness.

I can see you pondering – 'If I could create from such places what would I create?' Well, like everybody else, you do – from the multidimensional part of you that already vibrates and exists there.

I would like to help by connecting you to that part of ourself so 'you may explain more to yourself'. It is an aspect of your higher self arkarna and entity with a fluid energetic presentation of form.

**Creative Higher Self: CHS** (another attribute of higher self or a different higher self arkarna programme) In what form would you like me to present myself?

**R:** The form you wish. *(She comes forward as a fluctuating presentation containing all the people I am closely linked with – they are all part of higher self though there are several I do not know.)* One image has no more preference than another.

**CHS:** I have some images of our self.

**R:** *(She shows me Trito the Cytith.)*

**CHS:** Antemedi was trying to convey that *form is of no concern but to those that have concern about form*. To be here, one needs to be free from such concerns or comforts. There is nothing to comfort or not to comfort and those thoughts do not form part of this vibration. You may allow into your consciousness different forms and projections that suit the arkarnas of many dimensions and densities.

**R:** *(At this point I feel her all around and within me. What were her flickering lights and 'projection of forms' are now around me. What a strange feeling this is. I feel transformed as I become images of different body forms. Some bodies are just energy without the need to form, but others seem more solid or more explored.)*

**CHS:** Let us begin talking about what you were, are, and will be. These terms describe past, now and future and are relative to the appearance of movement. Soul creations are not informed by or restricted by those parameters, and at these levels of arkarna we talk about overarching other arkarnas. You might think that creativity requires some thought or thinking about creative possibilities. But it does not. Thought of this kind creates a boundary in a similar way to your database.

Here, every possible creation exists as a possibility. It does not need to be 'thought up', an arkarna can formulate possibilities by allowing possibilities within the framework of unbounded love and expression. The possibilities 'coalesce' from additional parameters and links with other souls' arkarnas. As the possibilities naturally adhere to one another they create timelines on lower dimensions. Possibilities are endless and any life force or field can be encountered or experienced.

As you focus on this energy you will see its 'vibratory fluctuations' and feel no need do anything. There is nothing to do and nothing to be. There are no needs to satisfy – you need not be satisfied. What comes – comes. Yet, it is not random, despite the wide variation in what can be evoked. Another word for creating is 'imagined into being'. As creators imagine.

So yes – it's made up – it's all made up. The very thing that you baulked against, wanting things to be real and not imaginary. The link between imagination and 'imagined into

**248**

being' was as if one was a truth and the other a lie. Here we could say there is only truth and no lies, but there are many variations of what is true. You cannot hold one aloft and say this is the ultimate truth because you might need to change it to fit an alternative situation. Everything is made up!

**R:** Wow – now that's a strange feeling. It's like everything is a lie – nothing is real only energies that can take different forms. There are no truths and there are no lies because they would restrict what is possible. It makes perfect sense in its rationale and irrationality. This puts Antemedi's introductory talk about truth in another dimension – literally!

**CHS:** So there you have it and only after a few words of communication! Truth does not exist in the way you think it does. Even to say the soul is *fluid energy* is a description so is that a truth? For you, truth is something that's immovable until further discovery means it can be revised to another monolithic statement. Your perception of truth does not accord with this realm.

**R:** I am just beginning to realise what that means: *I no longer need to search for the truth.* It is an intrinsic part of enlightenment but only to a certain point. It is also an appearance of progress until it is not. What we create on earth is only part of our arkarna program there or on that level. It is of little effect upon the soul at these levels. I am an experience of creating residual energies and the experience of clearing them up.

**CHS:** You are beginning to see that these new thoughts will free you from attachments. It is certainly a different perspective to see that nothing is real. You have been ascribing meaning to 'reality' as somehow existing on the truth side of 'truth and lies'. If you cannot find truth, can you find reality?

So is love real? It is certainly a created experience and one that we would prefer. As the soul creates this, we could say that it is real because it creates and expresses itself. But if it's all 'made up and created' that could be said 'not to be real'.

**R:** Mowhar again. Invent, imagine, create and make up. It no longer feels like an untruth or an unreality, so how do we define what is real and tangible internally? Certainly not by another person's external measure of truth! And to that question of Antemedi: "How do we know that the mantoids were not a creation of your imagination or ours?"

**HSC:** Well that demonstrates quite clearly that you were hearing it through the filter of 'what is truth?' when there should be no such filter. It challenged you and your thought: *It must be a truth I have seen them – they were introduced by my trusted guides and they gave some great information. It's got to be true it cannot be imagined.* When in fact the 'free flow' of imagination is part of creativity. We only reflected your doubts to yourself. There is no more in that question than that. It was a prompt as an intrinsic part of accepting these realisations.

There was no deeper meaning than the one we have given. What greater depth could there be than the one we have just shown you? Antemedi's question was meant to perplex you and if we can use the word, *truth* – that is the *truth* of it as a question.

Unless you are prepared to accept there is no 'definable' or 'ultimate' truth, it will restrict your access to certain levels of the Isness. Who wants to restrict unlimited potential to specific definitions of truth?

**R:** Understood. Thank you. *(Antemedi becomes the focal point.)*

**A:** Now things will begin to pick up a pace!

Keep with and around you the awareness of the fluctuating energetic body projections. This will help loosen your Robert sense of self. We will then be able to converse with 'less' between us. Take a pause with me before returning to the laptop.

**R:** (*During the pause, we spoke at depth and here is the summary*) Over the last few minutes, you explained there is no sense of ego-self while we exist and walk within that higher awareness; yet when I return to awareness in the earth arkarna, it seems the sense of self returns..

**A:** And so it does but you can choose how you let it affect you.

As to picking up a pace, let us proceed. My words flow as if they are free to be themselves – *you do not need to seek any truth within my words.* There are many readers who will now understand those words. Who would have thought it was possible to accept that their way is not to seek the truth in my words? Certainly there would have been a lot less at the beginning of this book.

'Tempaney – coowahlah – satenisay' basically means that energetic resonances are attached to words and their meanings – these will become known in due course.

**R:** We are quite some way into a growing word count; is there a book ending you have in mind?

**A:** Yes and yes, but there are a few more things we would like to cover so please concentrate on what I say it will help me to be more succinct.

When you speak with intent it will create energy; this can be projected to one or more individuals. This was shown in your meeting with the Arcturian Orators. I would like you to consider that you have a voice and it can convey energetic resonances. You think that when this book ends the effort will be sufficient and that the message is finished. That is your desire to be finished with the typing. But we have other information to convey over sequential events, so there will be more to type in the months ahead – everything in its place.

**R:** Okay, I will go with the flow but you know that already.

**A:** Yes – just a little mental preparation that as one thing ends another takes over.

Keep your awareness full within 'your other-selves energies'; that will anchor you more within those levels. That is a sound place from which 'to be'. There is nothing you have to do and there is no failure and no success.

**R:** Thank you, I understand what you are saying.

**A:** Let's take a moment to consider where things are heading. We have said much, though there is more to say. Our prime objective was to raise awareness of information that has not been explored in any great depth before. This, we believe, we have done in ways that can be grasped and understood. The ideas will raise other questions in the shallows and in the depths.

People have always had questions of themselves and many seek answers to the 'way of things' and their origins. This delivery is part of one of many similar communications from other entities. It coincides with the energetic changes around your planet. So as I say, everything in its place.

# NINE

Antemedi talks about removing reference points from our minds in order that they can be free and fluid. He explains that we can move forward without anticipation or precursors, but we have to be careful about what we wish to create. Robert stumbles forward in an old way of thinking distorting what he creates.

**Robert:** Last time, we spoke about creating form from energy.

**Antemedi:** You think there are some secrets we can give you?

**R:** No, I just didn't feel as though the topic was completed.

**A:** All in its time – there are no secrets, it's all about the nature of mind. Not what the mind is in control of, but how free it is with no parameters or lurking doubts.

Imagine a flat landscape with straight energetic lines in a grid pattern to give reference and scale. That's quite a straightforward concept of unlimited freedom until the lines start moving about. But if the mind is free, it has to be free from the reference points we have created. To cope with the moving lines you could impose your will and change them, but what would you change them to? This type of freedom does not fit your constructs, so you don't know what can be created from it.

Creation in freedom needs no reference points, so any helpful reference points are unhelpful. This is difficult for you because your mind still wants me to locate you, particularly when I know where I am taking you. You believe this will be easier because your logic says that if a path exists it must go somewhere – then it feels tangible.

In that way, you will have missed the point. This is about freeing your mind not following me.

**R:** What about our connected unification? *(You are me and I am you, so can we use that?)*

**A:** Doesn't work like that. Every part of us that wants to be free has to free itself. My guidance is always here for you but as a particular aspect of our mind, I cannot free another part of our mind which is self-autonomous. I can show you what your restrictions are and how to leave them but the choices are still yours.

If you are happy to make the choice let us step forward over the threshold and accept that this next vibrational level has no reference points not even to ourselves – there can't be.

Feel the completeness, the stillness and peacefulness. There is an abundance of energy here. If we give out a thought, it returns to fulfil our desires and sponsoring thoughts. If we think *colours,* we are immediately surrounded by colours of all shades. If we think *people,* we are surrounded by them. Whatever we think, the Isness provides.

**R:** I see what you meant earlier about reference points and their ability to restrict. The feeling here, while peaceful, is meaningless to human life. Past ways of thinking seem unfulfilling; it would be to have everything that we wanted created from a shallow repetition of the past. It would be welcome to have something out of the blue – different, not a remake from the same parameters.

**A:** In order to avoid a rehash, all thought parameters need to be dispensed with. Let us have no parameters so we can walk forward without 'expecting' or without 'not expecting' because either would be a parameter.

**R:** (We are moving through dangling tapes suspended high above. They remind me of cinema filmstrips because there are sequential pictures on each tape. We can look at any one of them and review the action.)

**A:** Thought becomes a deed and the outcome of the deed is energy. The filmstrips show potential scenarios that can be joined together to make the experiences you need. But these are still reflective of your existing database arkarna. You get more of the same because you haven't asked for anything different.

**R:** Okay, please let it change.

**A:** But that is still asking from your existing program.

**R:** Okay, then show me how not to.

**A:** That's the point I can't show you – I have already explained why that is.

**R:** Okay, let me use the power of thought. I am going to keep walking through this maze of ribbons until it ends and then I can see what is on the other side. *(After a while moving forwards I realise it's not going to end because my **intent is to keep walking**. I know what I wanted but I created competing thoughts within my statement.)* So I desire to stop walking and be free from the ribbons. I realise it's an exercise in seeing not only the power of the mind but of having clear thoughts and intent.

As the ribbons fade, we enter a grey cylindrical enclosure and we move into its centre. Light swirls around us and we float upwards. It's a liberating feeling but I get somewhat light-headed. New thoughts begin to fill missing places in my mind. I wonder *what is the point of desiring when it can only be fulfilled according to the desire, which is a parameter?* Can it be that to exceed or have no parameters, one should not even desire to

255

exceed them? Otherwise, the desire to exceed parameters becomes a reflection as well. Antemedi said expectations are parameters so that must mean desires are as well. What a strange place this is – in order to exist to its function one has to let go of all things – hope, love, satisfaction and the self. I am still all I was, but do I now exist as potential? I have no need to ignite any of the potentials that exist here.

Many times before, I would have felt comfortable standing in awe soaking up the wonderful energies. Those were limited and restricted appreciations, fleeting for only a few moments. The true nature unfolds – all is here ready to do my bidding in a different way. I am quite dumbfounded and I do not know what to desire. Is it even possible to live in such a way?

**Creative Higher Self:** You listen well to yourself – to the *me* of you. Most desires are for satisfaction or dissatisfaction. Some may say they desire knowledge for knowledge's sake, but that is to hide the satisfaction in learning more. Whatever label humanity wishes to put on its actions – it is a desire. To offer one's help or to selflessly save others is noble. But that, too, is a value system and those that are noble who may say they do not value their efforts, still do so because they devalue them, and that is the other side of duality – it is still a human desire.

There is no one on earth that does not have desires and who lives according to them. Antemedi said, "Any parameter or format that is directive, sponsors what you create." Yes, you may look at your desires in the context we have placed them and you might allow the needs of love to surpass desire. Remember, 'like comes to like' so all misunderstandings will return and show themselves in every moment.

So, desire – what next? It is, as you understand it. If you desire to see beyond desire' it still remains as desire. In which case, it is a conundrum.

**R:** Not desiring to have desire is a catch 22. Maybe it's another reflection of Mowhar. But desire, as you point out, is a basic human building block. I am not sure how or even if it is possible to live without desire.

**CHS:** That would be to observe and act to your observations without engaging desire. It is not a way that corresponds with your idea of life. It is another form of arkarna but it is also entity living as well. The fact that it is so removed from your ideals does not make it less worth living. We would not accept it unless it fulfilled our ideas of love. It is not possible for you to shed your desires while inhabiting a land of desires. In any event, would you really want to do that?

**R:** I can't think of a good reason, so why then are you showing this way of living and thinking? It doesn't seem to achieve much.

**CHS:** Achievement is, of course, desire and measurement. Does it have to achieve anything?

**R:** In your realm, perhaps not, but in mine we live very differently. This book is supposed to help to achieve an appreciation of different ways of thinking.

**CHS:** We are showing you a different way of thinking at the moment, but you can't see the benefit of it. It is of no benefit – it is beyond that. I am giving an explanation through the feeling of these concepts. If it can never be of benefit to you in the way that you see 'benefit', then it seems pointless.

**R:** Yes, a construct that seems to have little relevance here on earth.

**CHS:** But it has relevance here and to many other societies; it's not just a process of the higher self. On earth, everyone places emphasis on desire and gratification. Often it's been said that you seek something because you do not have it.

There are many states of being beyond gratification. Many beings you have encountered exist without the trauma of desires needing to be fulfilled.

Take a step within me and give no consideration to purpose or answers. We have no purpose and no function other than to be. There really is nothing else – we have no whimsical nature or anything to seek. We need nothing. Tranquillity is a word that could be used, but then again it stands in reference to that which is not. Here we have tranquillity, but it is not in reference to anything else.

**R:** This is very hard to grasp, but I would expect you to say there is nothing to grasp.

**CHS:** You have forgotten about the fluctuations within your aura, and you have slipped a little too much into Robert. Focus on the energy of your different expressions into soul in order to be more fully with me. Expect nothing and become at one with your other projections.

This is a place of all things and no-things. It is a place where you are many people and many projections. Our projections may have their desires on their dimensional levels, but we cannot have desire here because that would not allow our projections to have their freedoms.

**R:** But you were intimating that the freedom from desire is more desirable because of the trauma desire creates.

**CHS:** You create in your ways and we do here in ours. You create through desire, and we do not. We create for our whole self for each and every part of the fluctuating projections. Our desire would override yours if we were to function with it. The truth is we cannot function with it unless we are the projection.

You are beginning to see that desire has limitations and a degree of pointlessness. This is because your desires are having less relevance to your way of being. What about joy for the sake of joy? Joy not bound by fulfilling desires. Without 'random desire' you will not get pulled in all sorts of odd directions. Desire awareness is something different.

**R:** I am beginning to think this is too hard or just not possible to fully grasp. I hear and understand what you say, but there is a big disconnect somewhere, and this dialogue is unlikely to make easy reading.

**CHS:** So are we to put this right so that you may forgo your struggle? We cannot let desire get in the way.

**R:** Get in the way of what?

**A:** Let's try this by connecting more deeply with your fluctuations. Connect with all the expressions in your aura and, when calm and connected, listen without the desire to understand.

**CHS:** At this level, we can see our projections having their desires fulfilled without our need to be involved. We experience pleasure that they may have their desires fulfilled. We have joy in seeing what we have created as you, and what has created itself within the arkarnas. Our expressions into forms are varied. Those like Orlacka undertake life in loving responsibility without desire taking a heavy hand. Here, responsibility does not exist because that is a function of desire. There is the joy in allowing and watching and being with others who are similar. There are many others who allow creation and create without desire.

We can rejoice in being at one with ourselves and our like-minded souls. It is splendid without comparison because it has no need for desire – it is wondrous. You could say that our desires are fulfilled in totality to the point that we have no need for them. It is a state of being and it is not temporary and neither sustainable nor unsustainable. It is wonder without bounds. We can stretch across many lands and more.

The arkarnas at this level do as they do yet we are still entities. We are you beyond the constraint for desire and its expression. So feel this feeling as best you can. We are individual entities as well as one entity we are you. There is no preference to be in one focus or another – to be an individual or the greater oneness. It is a joy to be and share and love with no ifs or buts.

**R:** Thank you, I am encapsulated by some of those feelings and now get a small glimpse of what it might be like here. Joy and completeness without desire. This is a much deeper feeling and makes more sense as a way of being. It's neither my feelings obscured nor a temporary touch on the outside surface of this inner realm. It's the inside as best can be seen and felt.

I know for my living on earth this moment shall still be a temporary experience, but this level doesn't feel distant anymore. It is not untouchable in unknowingness. There is a feeling to this belonging. I feel equivalent to higher self with no value system in the way. I am one of my experiences, which is beyond value.

**CHS:** Then we have joy in your joy, which is my joy that I feel within me – you may return to desire as much as you wish.

**R:** Thank you.

# TEN

Antemedi reflects on an ending summation that does not end.

**A:** You think we had better start summing up and putting an order and context to things. But there never was going to be an end because the spiritual universe cannot be tidied and boxed-up complete.

Does it go on forever? Well, that depends on what it is. For the soul, there is no end because there was no beginning – no before. There are certainly many ways to describe or see the same things so description goes on. Everyone will have a different take on what we have said and there will be topics that they find more interesting or more compelling than others.

What is heard and understood of all that's given is another matter. It's more about where people are at 'in their head' and what they are going through. What's being received from us is superimposed on existing measurement systems so what people get will vary enormously.

We don't think a synopsis is actually a very good thing because it would take snippets out of context and diminish the depths of feelings generated by the full metaphors. If an item is of that much interest, it can always be re-read.

**R:** Not the summing up I was expecting.

**A:** Very rarely can you see what I say in advance. You feel we are coming to a flat ending as if the tap has been turned off. That is certainly not so for you because we will continue with our communications as usual. You are musing on the potential for a more dramatic or uplifting ending. Even you do not listen to my words without the interference of desire. In my first line above, I said it would not end – so how then could I provide an uplifting ending?

**R:** An uplifting partial ending.

**A:** But it's not even partial, it continues. I can't stop being who I am or what I become and neither can you or the readers. We don't end.

**R:** But you take my point this book will end; it can't continue.

**A:** Of course I do, your typing needs to leave the laptop. Look to what I reflected about endings and read it again.

**R:** Forever appreciated.

**A:** That is the way of things when seen without the constraint of time.

There are a couple of things I would like to offer for consideration at this stage. The practices I have outlined at the beginning of this submission do not need to be entertained for an individual to progress. How each of you develops, or at what rate, will fit in with life's demands and interests. There is no *have to* or *should do,* the life of soul expression isn't based on what someone else says you should do. Life, its growth, and love are presented daily in everyone's personal arkarna, even if the multidimensional connections are ignored.

There is no guilt attached to how evolved anyone should be, and after all, who should set the standards and measurements? That would be yet another reflection of the way humanity thinks. Guilt is an imposed internal and external form of judgement and pain. It is used as a means, as a driving force for apparent good or change. Though cause and effect return your created energy in very diverse ways.

There are changing influences upon your societies and there

is a lot more hidden dirty washing that needs to come out. There will be pressures from those currently holding power who ignore their guardianship of others. It would be magnificent if you were no longer under the yolk of indoctrination. That would be freethinking to the level of your arkarna. There is no escape or running away that is to misunderstand and not see you are trying to run away from yourself. Changing your thoughts and arkarnas is neither easy or hard it is only a measurement that you make of possibilities.

We have shown you different ways of thinking but if I can leave you with anything, it would be to believe in yourself. It could be that you could exceed belief in yourself and live beyond belief or the need to believe and not be frightened of fear. But that is the reality of my world, which is not the same as yours.

Many different ways of thinking will be beyond you at present but the pathways are open if you want to explore.

Not many have full sight or belief in who and what they are. You are all free thinkers if that's your wish – it's just a matter of which *WAY* you wish to think and what will suit you best.

# Glossary

An explanation of some of the more common terms used throughout *Consciousness and the Alien Mind*

**Non-space/no space:**

**Access interface to knowledge**: The ability to understand information in a context without the need to reference it to other information. Information that does not need to be compared in order understand its fullness. While it can be the knowledge from past experience, it is more the 'coming into existence of knowledge' being able to just know. This can be done on energetic metal levels with or without technology enhancement. It shouldn't be forgotten that information is part of the construction of the universe as well as the souls within it. The two are inseparable so universal information is an intrinsic part of a higher dimensional being.

**Arcturians:** Humanoids from the planets surrounding the star Arcturus in the Bootes constellation. Their body forms are sustained by light and they are active in several different dimensions. A highly evolved benevolent race.

**Andromedans:** Humanoids of many different types from the Andromedan galaxy. With or without hair and different coloured skin tones and body sizes, they exist on many planets in their galaxy and beyond. They have huge biospheres several miles across which can relocate in different parts of the universe. An evolved benevolent race.

**Arkarna Programs:** A generic term for an interactive entity program that has many facets or attributes. Programs are an intrinsic part of the universe and soul. Arkarnas work at different vibrations with different parameters for different levels of awareness. They are involved in function and form as well as a determination of the type of interface between minds and beings. The arkarnas are a part of us and we of them. They are the underlying ethos and expression of the universe.

**Dimensional vibrational pockets:** When dimensional blending alters and a dimension vibrates faster, some of the original lower vibrations can still exist. However, they do so in their own dimensional pockets. They coagulate in pockets but they do not have access to the upgraded vibration. They can access each other's vibration through non-space and exist in the same space. To you it will be as if they are not there because they cannot interface beyond their own boundaries. Eventually these pockets will disappear because like attracts like.

**Essence energy:** Used as another term for etheric or auric being the information and emotion energy that underlies the appearance of form seen as matter. In effect, it's what you would see at another dimension level if the physical form were removed.

**Flux:** Another term for pulse energy but one that may have modulations or slight variations to the rates of pulse.

**Harmonies:** Created from pulse and information. The energetic harmonies or bubbles interact with each other in accordance with the information fields. An energy burst occurs where they interact which becomes the basic energetic representation or form in that dimension.

**Higher vibrational densities:** A term that can cover several things. In the main, a lower vibration will feel heavier or denser when compared to a higher density vibration. The higher density will have a faster vibration, which will be less restrictive and much lighter. Higher vibrational densities can also mean the same thing as a higher vibrational dimension but it depends on context. However a higher vibrational dimension can still have a variation of faster or slower vibrations relative to that dimension.

**Humanoid:** A simple term that gives a large degree of similarity to form and shape, mostly two legs two arms and eyes. Often there may be DNA similarities of some kind. DNA also exists as a form of vibration which can be viewed as information, This information exists throughout the universe and is one reason for similarities. In addition, genetical manipulation and creation of humans is undertaken by other beings. The vibrational and physical DNA information is able to adapt to the arkarnas of particular environments.

**Information Fields:** Part of the construct of matter pertinent to each vibrational dimension. It is information that gives instruction to pulse energy in order to create harmonies. Alternatively, you may view it as the information being filled with pulse. The information remains as is but it alters to the requirements of any arkarnas that have programs of movement or change. Advanced beings can also use technology to alter information to transform their environments.

**Isness:** That which *is* as opposed to that which *is not* or that which never came about. It is a universal structure that requires nothing and has no needs – it is a function of itself. It will reflect back to you what you show it and place no value upon interaction with it. It is purity of vibrational energy. It is a vibrational place where all things are at one beyond even the need for harmony or balance. If you have read Isness in the main text it will be within a context that gives it a feeling. The feeling of Isness is important to understanding it. It is not an easy concept for us to be at one with and appreciate its deeper understandings.

**Light being:** A generic term for a being that vibrates or resonates at high frequency. When viewed from our lower vibrations we see them more as light even though they have a form. Light beings will be more fluid than our own form and exist cognisant in several dimensions.

**Mantoid:** A being that looks like a mantis but seems to have elements that we would associate with humanoid. (I have the same mantoid from earlier with me while I am explaining this particular term.) He says, "Humans have elements that are similar to them – surely it's all a matter of perspective and who compares who to whom?"

**Mowhar:** Start or original creation energy. Paradoxically, it came from nothing and something at the same time. Like opposites that cancelled each other out but never existed until they did.

Something that does not exist in our terms yet to our mind it exists as nothing. Like infinity and limitlessness. it is difficult for us to conceive nothingness from our constructs.

**Pulse energy:** Is also described at times as on-pulse and off-pulse, which are the states of the dimensional energies as it pulses or fluxes.

# References

## ONE
[1] Students of Life: (p2)
   www.roblomax.co.uk/students-of-life/
[2] Plausibility: (p6)
   www.roblomax.co.uk/plausability/
[3] Cytith Aquatic Humanoid: (p47)
   www.roblomax.co.uk/cytith-aquatic-humanoid/
[4] Second Meeting Cytith: (p47)
   www.roblomax.co.uk/second-meeting-cytith/


## TWO
[5] Antemedi Andromedan perspective 6: (p77)
   https://youtu.be/YJcnAGCsbol
[6] Antemedi Andromedan perspective 7: (p77)
   https://youtu.be/yCnkoP9tc_A

## THREE
[7] The Boy, the Beast and the Nothingness: (p97)
   https://www.youtube.com/watch?v=-ZUZb7uyJZA

**Note:** *Full coloured renditions of the greyscale images used in this book can be seen on the landing page* **https://www.roblomax.co.uk**

# About the author

Robert Lomax lives in Norfolk, England, and considers himself to be a normal family man. However, when his third child, Ralph, died in a tragic accident, aged nine months, it caused him to reconsider the values that society imposes upon us. In the aftermath of that devastating loss, his childhood psychic abilities were reawakened and he regained his passion for painting.

This invigorated spiritual contact allowed him to spend more than two-and-a-half decades quietly working away with his spirit guides, looking at his existing thought-processes in the context of self and beyond.

Throughout this period, he has given his time freely to help bereaved people and provide spiritual healing to others. Whenever possible, he continues to do this alongside his near daily channelling and writing. This, however, is the first time his close spiritual contacts have helped him construct a book containing some of their alien insights.

As with all of Robert's previous written articles and drawings, this book is free over the internet. Any royalties from the printed version will be used to promote alien messages from his spirit guides. Robert and his wife have three grown up sons, daughters-in-law and a first grandchild.

Visit Robert's website to find out more:
**www.roblomax.co.uk**

Lightning Source UK Ltd.
Milton Keynes UK
UKHW022147141019
351604UK00006B/279/P